Cambridge Elements ≡

Elements in Histories of Emotions and the Senses
edited by
Jan Plamper
University of Limerick

T0286999

MAKING NOISE IN THE MODERN HOSPITAL

Victoria Bates
University of Bristol

CAMBRIDGE
UNIVERSITY PRESS

CAMBRIDGE
UNIVERSITY PRESS

University Printing House, Cambridge CB2 8BS, United Kingdom

One Liberty Plaza, 20th Floor, New York, NY 10006, USA

477 Williamstown Road, Port Melbourne, VIC 3207, Australia

314–321, 3rd Floor, Plot 3, Splendor Forum, Jasola District Centre, New Delhi – 110025, India

103 Penang Road, #05–06/07, Visioncrest Commercial, Singapore 238467

Cambridge University Press is part of the University of Cambridge.

It furthers the University's mission by disseminating knowledge in the pursuit of education, learning, and research at the highest international levels of excellence.

www.cambridge.org
Information on this title: www.cambridge.org/9781108813662
DOI: 10.1017/9781108885010

© Victoria Bates 2021

First published 2021

A catalogue record for this publication is available from the British Library.

ISBN 978-1-108-81366-2 Paperback
ISSN 2632-1068 (online)
ISSN 2632-105X (print)

Making Noise in the Modern Hospital

Elements in Histories of Emotions and the Senses

DOI: 10.1017/9781108885010
First published online: November 2021

Victoria Bates
University of Bristol

Author for correspondence: Victoria Bates, victoria.bates@bristol.ac.uk

Abstract: This Element examines the problem of hospital noise, a problem that has repeatedly been discovered anew, with each new era bringing its own efforts to control and abate unwanted sound in healthcare settings. Why, then, has hospital noise never been resolved? This question is at the heart of *Making Noise in the Modern Hospital*, which brings together histories of the senses, space, technology, society, medicine and architecture to understand the changing cacophony of the late twentieth-century British hospital. This Element is fundamentally interdisciplinary – despite being historical, it comes up to the present day and brings in scholarship on space, place, atmosphere and the senses that will have relevance to scholars working outside of historical research. The intersection between medical and sensory histories also puts interdisciplinary research at the Element's core.

Keywords: hospitals, NHS, noise, sound, space

ISBNs: 9781108813662 (PB), 9781108885010 (OC)
ISSNs: 2632-1068 (online), 2632-105X (print)

Contents

Introduction

In June 1962, W. R. Lang was hit by a collapsing wall when walking along a street in York.[1] The injured patient was taken to the local hospital and eventually 'wheeled into a big ward, ready for a comfortable bed and a sleep … for if one can't rest in a hospital where can one expect to find peace?' Unfortunately, Lang complained, 'I was in for a rude shock. A National Health Service hospital is the last place in Britain to find quiet.'[2] This account was published in *Q[uiet] P[lease]: The Journal of the Noise Abatement Society*, a society launched in 1959 to combat the 'noise pollution' problem. The Noise Abatement Society reported on a range of perceived problem areas, from hospitals to traffic, and successfully lobbied for the 1960 Noise Abatement Act that classed noise as a 'statutory nuisance'. It was part of a wider contemporary concern about noise, 'modernity' and urban life. The government established a Committee on the Problem of Noise, which published a white paper on the issue in 1963.[3] Letters from the public flooded this committee, complaining about a wide range of themes, including noise problems that were apparently new – or increasing – with technological change such as traffic, aircraft and loudspeakers.[4] The hospital was one of many sites discussed as part of this flurry of public and parliamentary interest in combatting 'noise pollution'.

The hospital noise that Lang bemoaned might, then, not be viewed as a problem of particular note. However, the hospital had significance in these debates. Considering the wide range of 'noise' problems in modern Britain, including many busy and high-technology spaces, the particular and continued attention paid to hospitals over the course of the post-war period is noteworthy. In 1955, the Nuffield Trust health charity complained that '[f]or the last quarter of a century hospitals have been becoming steadily noisier … knowing the causes of the present situation has not pointed to any simple cure'.[5] A letter to the *British Medical Journal* (*BMJ*) over two decades later, in 1978, praised 'a timely report on the increasing menace of noise … rapidly growing in our hospitals'.[6] *The Journal of the Noise Abatement Society* repeatedly returned to hospitals as case studies, with articles written from the perspectives of patients and staff alike. The society even ran a 'Noise Control in Hospitals' competition in the 1970s for sites that had successfully tackled the

---

[1] W. R. Lang, 'Our Noisy Hospitals!', *QP: The Journal of the Noise Abatement Society*, 1:4 (1962), 26.
[2] Lang, 'Our Noisy Hospitals!', 26.
[3] Alan Wilson, *Noise: Final Report [of the] Committee on the Problem of Noise* (HM Stationery Office, 1963).
[4] The National Archives, London, 'Committee on the Problem of Noise: From Public', MH 146/32; The National Archives, London, 'Noise in Hospitals', MH 146/44.
[5] Nuffield Provincial Hospitals Trust, *Studies in the Functions and Design of Hospitals* (Oxford University Press, 1955), p. 115.
[6] H. A. Fleming, 'Points from Letters: Hospital Noise', *British Medical Journal*, 1:6105 (1978), 115.

problem.[7] The history of hospital noise deserves attention in its own right and should not just be subsumed into a wider story of noise abatement.

Hospital noise was repeatedly discussed as a 'growing', or even a 'new' or 'neglected', problem during this period. In 1953, for example, *The Lancet* reported on a memorandum by the Central Health Services Council that bemoaned 'how little thought is nowadays given to noise in hospitals'.[8] This neglect apparently compared unfavourably with previous centuries, when hospital noise 'was, of course, a matter to which Miss Nightingale gave a good deal'.[9] This comment about 'Miss Nightingale' is a reference to the famous nurse Florence Nightingale, who wrote extensively on hospital environments and the importance of colour, light, air and peace for recovery. Implicitly, this article referred to her famous quote in *Notes on Nursing* (1859): 'Unnecessary noise . . . is the most cruel absence of care which can be inflicted either on sick or well.'[10] The history of concerns about hospital noise also pre-dates these famous words. As Karin Bijsterveld notes '[t]he notion that the ill deserved tranquillity had a . . . long history' going back to antiquity, with solutions over the centuries ranging from relocating patients away from noise sources to putting straw on pavements outside hospitals.[11] The longer history of ideas about sound and health is an important backdrop to the discussion that follows. 'Noise' could only be constructed as a problem in hospitals when there was a belief in the value of peace and quiet. The origins of this belief are deep-rooted. Some of the earliest hospitals were entwined with churches, abbeys and priories; as Keir Waddington notes in relation to the medieval years of St Bartholomew's Hospital, at this point they often focused on 'medicine for the soul'.[12] In such a spiritual-medical framework of thought, inner and outer peace were inextricably interwoven.

The Lancet was right to note that there was a long history to concerns about hospital noise. It was on shakier ground, though, with its implicit claim that the noise problem had been forgotten between the 1850s and 1950s. In the 1930s, campaigns against hospital noise had been led by the Anti-Noise League, a spiritual predecessor of the Noise Abatement Society that was concerned about urban sound and industrial modernity. It had even curated an exhibition on 'dealing with hospital noises' and published a leaflet entitled 'Hospitals:

---

[7] Wellcome Library, London, 'Records of the Noise Abatement Society', SA/NAS (uncatalogued), accession number 2131.

[8] Anon., 'The Patient in His Hospital', *The Lancet*, 261:6753 (1953), 227–8.

[9] Anon., 'The Patient'.

[10] Florence Nightingale, *Notes on Nursing* (Harrison & Sons, 1859), p. 31.

[11] Karin Bijsterveld, *Mechanical Sound: Technology, Culture, and Public Problems of Noise in the Twentieth Century* (MIT Press, 2008), p. 62.

[12] Keir Waddington, *Medical Education at St. Bartholomew's Hospital, 1123–1995* (Boydell & Brewer, 2003), p. 13.

Planning against Noise'.[13] Interest in the topic of hospital noise waxed and waned in line with general noise abatement campaigns, but it was a stretch to claim that 'little thought' was given to the topic. *The Lancet* article might be better thought of as part of a genre, in which hospital noise was repeatedly identified as a particular, contemporary problem. This trend continues to this day, as does the tendency for such writings to look nostalgically to the past as a time of apparent relative quiet and calm in hospitals.[14] One *BMJ* blog, for example, recently referred to Sylvia Plath's 1961 poem 'Tulips' and its description of peace in hospital as now 'antiquated and implausible'.[15] In the light of the earlier cited complaints, it is ironic to see the post-war period cited as a period of relative peace in hospitals.

It seems that the problem of hospital noise was repeatedly discovered anew, with each new era bringing its own efforts to control and abate unwanted sound in healthcare settings. If this was indeed the case, why has hospital noise never been resolved? This question is at the heart of this Element, which examines hospital cacophonies and the making of 'noise' in the National Health Service (NHS), the British public healthcare system launched in 1948.[16] It suggests that one answer may lie in changes to the soundscape itself. The twentieth-century hospital environment was bombarded with new sounds, including more people, the rise of traffic on streets outside, the acoustic qualities of new construction materials and emerging healthcare technologies such as alarms and monitors. However, this is not the full story. A more complex picture emerges when 'noise' is also understood in social and cultural terms. 'Noise', as a socially constructed concept, was not simply a growing problem that hospitals failed to tackle. It was repeatedly *reinvented* as a different problem, or a number of different problems simultaneously, over the course of the twentieth century. Noise has been a constant problem to be tackled in hospitals because sounds – and the meanings of sounds – have changed constantly: when one noise problem in the hospital was tackled, another one emerged.

The late twentieth century might not be an obvious focal point for historians studying either noise or noise abatement. 'Modernity' is often linked to specific noisy environments, such as urban and industrial spaces, but was also marked by

---

[13] Anon., 'Noiseless Hospitals', *British Medical Journal*, 1:3917 (1936), 220.

[14] In 2018, for example, the *BMJ* published an editorial on 'noise pollution in hospitals' which – although acknowledging that it was not new – identified noise as 'a steadily worsening problem'; Andreas Xyrichis, John Wynne, Jamie Mackrill, Anne Marie Rafferty and Angus Carlyle, 'Noise Pollution in Hospitals', *British Medical Journal* (2018), 363:k4808.

[15] Estelle Jobson, 'Engaging with Patients on the Hospital Soundscape', 19 November 2018, https://blogs.bmj.com/bmj/2018/11/19/estelle-jobson-engaging-patients-hospital-soundscape/ (accessed: 25 January 2021).

[16] 'The NHS' is used here as an umbrella term, though in practice it refers to multiple healthcare systems. The NHS name applies to the systems of Great Britain: England, Scotland and Wales. Northern Ireland's system is called 'Health and Social Care' (HSC) but is often discussed in terms of the broad UK 'NHS' umbrella and was also launched in 1948..

the increasing control of noise internationally as part of a perceived process of civilisation. Historians looking for noisy spaces have therefore often studied the more distant past: one recent survey, *Cultural Histories of Noise, Sound and Listening in Europe*, for example, covers the period 1300–1918.[17] Historians interested in the *decline* of noisy spaces, or the making of sensory order, have tended to focus on the sensibilities of 'modernity' from the eighteenth century to the early twentieth century.[18] Few histories of noise abatement reach into the late twentieth century: Jon Agar's work on the medicalisation of noise relates to 'campaigns against noise from the 1860s to the 1930s'; Emily Thompson writes on reverberant sound and space in the early twentieth century; Peter Payer's article on 'The Age of Noise' in Vienna focuses on the period 1870–1914; and James G. Mansell's book on noise and 'modernity' declares 1914–45 to be 'the age of noise in Britain'.[19] There are some exceptions to this trend: for example, the work of Karin Bijsterveld covers most of the twentieth century; Jennifer Stoever writes on noise in post-war New York; and Sandra Jasper explores noise abatement in West Berlin.[20] In general, though, the late twentieth century is relatively neglected in this scholarship, especially with regard to British history. This period has great significance for the revival of noise abatement campaigns in politics, society and health. As Matthew Gandy notes, there was a 'growing ambivalence towards urban noise ... as a symbol of progress and prosperity, a disorienting and potentially health threatening source of social disorder, or a fascinating realm of cultural experimentation'.[21] There is a strong case that noise was, if anything, a *growing* concern over the course of the twentieth century.

This study is primarily about NHS hospitals in post-war England, for which there is the richest source material on hospital noise, but its scope extends across the late twentieth century and into Scotland and Wales.[22] It focuses on general

---

[17] Ian Biddle and Kirsten Gibsen, eds, *Cultural Histories of Noise, Sound and Listening in Europe, 1300–1918* (Routledge, 2016).

[18] An example for the earlier period is Peter Denney, Bruce Buchan, David Ellison and Karen Crawley, eds, *Sound, Space and Civility in the British World, 1700–1850* (Routledge, 2019).

[19] Jon Agar, 'Bodies, Machines and Noise' in Iwan Rhys Morus, ed., *Bodies/Machines* (Berg, 2002), p. 199; James G. Mansell, *The Age of Noise in Britain: Hearing Modernity* (University of Illinois Press, 2017); Peter Payer, 'The Age of Noise: Early Reactions in Vienna, 1870–1914', *Journal of Urban History*, 33:5 (2007), 773–93; Emily Thompson, *The Soundscape of Modernity: Architectural Acoustics and the Culture of Listening in America, 1900–1933* (MIT Press, 2002).

[20] Bijsterveld, *Mechanical Sound*; Sandra Jasper, 'Sonic Refugia: Nature, Noise Abatement and Landscape Design in West Berlin', *The Journal of Architecture*, 23:6 (2018), 36–60; Jennifer Stoever, '"Just Be Quiet Pu-leeze": The New York Amsterdam News Fights the Postwar "Campaign against Noise"', *Radical History Review*, 2015:121 (2015), 145–68.

[21] Matthew Gandy, 'Introduction', in Matthew Gandy and B. J. Nilsen, eds, *The Acoustic City* (Jovis, 2014), p. 10.

[22] Northern Ireland is not discussed in this Element, as there is not space to do justice to the differences in systems and provision, but it is worth noting that Altnagelvin was surveyed by the King's Fund for their hospital music trial.

hospitals, including general teaching hospitals, because of their importance as sites for a wide range of different types of treatment and care, from emergency to maternity and psychiatry. Such spaces have always been complex and contradictory. They provide excellent case studies of the 'ambivalence' identified by Gandy and how it shaped the definition, measurement and management of 'unnecessary' sound. Ideas of scientific modernity and medical efficiency were built into these healthcare spaces, to be both prized and critiqued, as were 'high technology' environments. Hospitals were also seen as *ideally* crucial spaces of rest and recuperation, even if this was not always the case in reality. Noise was essential to modern medicine, but its reduction was – to quote *The Guardian* in 1961 – desirable for creating a 'restful atmosphere'.[23] In the light of these tensions around necessary and unnecessary sound, it is perhaps unsurprising that hospitals were a common focus of noise abatement campaigns in Britain and internationally.[24]

The launch of the NHS in 1948 provides a unique opportunity to understand how 'noise' connected to a set of specific medical, social, political, economic and technological concerns. Noise was rediscovered and redefined as a problem in relation to new issues raised by the NHS, including concerns about efficiency, welfare and healthcare principles, and rebuilding for a general population. The NHS hospital can be viewed as a microcosm of wider changes happening in mid-to-late twentieth-century Britain. It was also a very specific kind of social space that brought together members of society who might never usually have mixed, grouping patients along specific lines such as age and illness. Hospitals brought with them power relations that were not found beyond their walls, as well as – with illness – new embodied and emotional relationships to space and place. The hospital as a case study thus offers layers. It brings together general social, technological and architectural trends. It also offers insights into the *specific* spatiality of a site that has been important to many people's lives in the modern world and that is still poorly understood.

There is extensive scholarship on the history of hospital buildings as a launching point for wider examinations of architecture, healthcare, welfare, medicine, politics, economics and modernity.[25] However, there is only a very

---

[23] Anon., 'End Washing Up Noises in Hospitals', *The Guardian*, 1 March 1961, 10.

[24] Some – of many – international news reports on hospital noise include Anon., 'Hinges Oiled', *The Jerusalem Post*, 5 September 1966, 4; Anon., 'Noise in Hospitals', *Chicago Daily Tribune*, 24 March 1958, 22; Anon., 'Noise Near Hospital', *South China Morning Post*, 13 July 1960, 2.

[25] For example, Annmarie Adams, *Medicine by Design: The Architect and the Modern Hospital, 1893–1943* (University of Minnesota Press, 2008); Irena Benyovsky Latin, Jane L. Stevens Crawshaw and Kathleen Vongsathorn, eds, *Tracing Hospital Boundaries: Integration and Segregation in Southeastern Europe and Beyond, 1050–1970* (Brill, 2020); Jeanne Kisacky, *Rise of the Modern Hospital: An Architectural History of Health and Healing, 1870–1940* (University of Pittsburgh Press, 2017); Charles E. Rosenberg, *The Care of Strangers: The Rise*

limited amount of work on the NHS hospital, and existing scholarship tends to deal more with architectural form than with questions of habitation and experience.[26] The lens of 'noise' broadens and adds to these existing hospital histories in two main ways. First, noise management goes beyond structured planning processes, to include more ad hoc acoustic design such as new materials or adjustments to layouts. Not only did new hospital architecture reflect changing healthcare principles but healthcare principles were also formed *through* adaptations to buildings and responses to problems. Second, histories of acoustic design and noise control show the value of shifting the focus of hospital history from how a building looked to how it felt.

The work that follows is not the first to explore 'noise' in healthcare settings, but it is the first to do so in depth, through an interdisciplinary lens and in relation to the NHS hospital. There is some fantastic existing historiography on the subject, but it tends to take the form of relatively short articles on specific issues: Katherine Fennelly writes on noise in early nineteenth-century asylums, David Theodore considers noise in relation to hospital architecture, Hillel Schwartz examines earplugs and Jonathan Reinarz writes (for a slightly earlier period) on senses and hospital visitors.[27] Other scholars of hospital history have paid some attention to noise and acoustic design, but typically as part of bigger studies rather than worthy of close examination in its own right; Annmarie Adams examines noise control in her work on early twentieth-century hospital architecture, for example, and Clare Hickman examines the senses in relation to

---

of *America's Hospital System* (Basic Books, 1987); Christine Stevenson, *Medicine and Magnificence: British Hospital and Asylum Architecture, 1660–1815* (Yale University Press, 2000); Stephen Verderber and David J. Fine, *Healthcare Architecture in an Era of Radical Transformation* (Yale University Press, 2000); Cor Wagenaar, ed., *The Architecture of Hospitals* (NAi Publishers, 2006); Julie Willis, Philip Goad and Cameron Logan, *Architecture and the Modern Hospital: Nosokomeion to Hygeia* (Routledge, 2019).

[26] Harriet Richardson, ed., *English Hospitals, 1660–1948: A Survey of Their Architecture and Design* (RCHME, 1998), goes up to 1948 but includes many of the hospitals inherited by the NHS. Books and articles specifically on NHS form and architecture include Alistair Fair, '"Modernization of Our Hospital System": The National Health Service, the Hospital Plan, and the "Harness" Programme, 1962–77', *Twentieth Century British History*, 29:4 (2018), 547–75; Rosemary Glanville, Ann Noble and Peter Scher, *50 Years of Ideas in Health Care Buildings* (Nuffield Trust, 1999); Jonathan Hughes, 'The "Matchbox on a Muffin": The Design of Hospitals in the Early NHS', *Medical History*, 44:1 (2000), 21–56; David Theodore, 'Treating Architectural Research: The Nuffield Trust and the Post-war Hospital', *The Journal of Architecture*, 24:7 (2019), 982–98.

[27] Katherine Fennelly, 'Out of Sound, Out of Mind: Noise Control in Early Nineteenth-Century Lunatic Asylums in England and Ireland', *World Archaeology*, 46:3 (2014), 416–30; David Theodore, 'Sound Medicine: Studying the Acoustic Environment of the Modern Hospital, 1870–1970', *The Journal of Architecture*, 23:6 (2018), 986–1002; Hillel Schwartz, 'Inner and Outer Sancta: Earplugs and Hospitals', in Trevor Pinch and Karin Bijsterveld, eds, *The Oxford Handbook of Sound Studies* (Oxford University Press, 2012), pp. 273–97; Jonathan Reinarz, 'Learning to Use Their Senses: Visitors to Voluntary Hospitals in Eighteenth-Century England', *Journal for Eighteenth-Century Studies*, 35:4 (2012), 505–20.

the history of hospital gardens, but noise is not the focus of either work.[28] In general, in fact, sound and noise are relatively under-explored in histories of architecture and specific built environments, despite the popularity of sound studies in urban history.[29] As Sabine von Fischer and Olga Touloumi note in their introduction to a rare special issue on the subject: '[d]espite its ubiquity, sound is largely missing from histories of architecture and the built environment'.[30] The significance of this research thus extends beyond the hospital, and offers a case study for an emerging field of enquiry.

This Element makes steps towards a spatially informed sensory history. It opens by unpicking the changing 'soundscape' of the NHS hospital. Its first section attempts to hear the NHS hospital in its full cacophony and to under-stand historical relationships between sound, built environments, people and objects. This analysis approaches sound as a productive process, rather than taking 'noise' as a stable object of study, and emphasises that no sound inherently carries the quality of being *noisy*. The first section closes by offering some ways in which historians might productively engage with the concept of 'atmospheres' in order to make some order out of disorderly cacophonies. It thus connects to wider bodies of literature in fields such as anthropology and geography on the senses, emotions and place-making.[31] Very little of this work has yet informed sensory histories, which have tended to focus on the social and cultural aspects of sound.

The second section turns more directly to the question of 'noise'. It shows that noise was defined and tackled as a problem in part by how it was measured, and multiple definitions of noise could co-exist. People who quantified noise, using new devices such as noise meters, tended to construct it as a problem of loudness and lean towards material solutions. Those researchers who used qualitative tools, such as questionnaires, tended instead to focus on social definitions of 'noise' and related behavioural solutions. This discussion builds on and develops some important recent histories of technology, which empha-sise the importance of measurement in the making of sound, space and place.[32] It also has much to contribute to wider social histories and sensory

---

[28] Adams, *Medicine by Design*, pp. 112–17; Clare Hickman, *Therapeutic Landscapes: A History of English Hospital Gardens since 1800* (Manchester University Press, 2013).

[29] For example, Alexander Cowan and Jill Steward, eds, *The City and the Senses: Urban Culture since 1500* (Ashgate Publishing Ltd, 2007).

[30] It is possible to find examples to counter this claim, but it is true that the field has been traditionally 'ocularcentric'; Sabine von Fischer and Olga Touloumi, 'Sound Modernities: Histories of Media and Modern Architecture', *The Journal of Architecture*, 23:6 (2018), 873.

[31] For example, Tim Ingold, *The Perception of the Environment: Essays on Livelihood, Dwelling and Skill* (Psychology Press, 2000); Mark Paterson and Martin Dodge, eds, *Touching Space, Placing Touch* (Routledge, 2012).

[32] For example, Bijsterveld, *Mechanical Sound*; Thompson, *The Soundscape of Modernity*.

anthropologies, which have long been interested in the changing cultures of specific sounds and the definitions of noise.[33] Such scholarship emphasises that the meanings of sounds are context-specific.[34] The hospital further demonstrates how the specific medical, social, cultural, political and economic contexts of healthcare shaped the category of 'noise' over time. Overall, this Element does not claim that hospitals were newly noisy in the post-war period, nor that it was new for hospital noise to be experienced in social and cultural terms during this time. It takes the late twentieth century as a period of change, which allows a close examination of the ways in which the 'same' problem (noise) was in practice always being remade.

1 Cacophony

Historians of modernity have long noted – in the words of Sophia Rosenfeld – that 'as the Western soundscape changed ... the uses of hearing, the meaning invested in sound, modes of aural attention, and conflict over the noises of everyday life all evolved accordingly'.[35] Hospital soundscapes were no different and we can learn much from the 'conflict over the noises of everyday life' in hospitals, which provide an opportunity to look in close detail at how and why 'noises' came to be labelled as such. The first part of Rosenfeld's point should not be rapidly skipped past in order to consider 'meaning' and 'conflict', however. It is important to start with the soundscape itself. This section seeks first to hear the hospital, before turning to explore which sounds came to be defined as 'noise', why, and to what end. It unpicks the different layers and scales of the hospital cacophony, showing that there are no neat narratives of the NHS hospital getting 'more' or 'less' noisy.

The term 'soundscape' is most famously rooted in the work of R. Murray Schafer, who used it in relation to acoustic ecology, but its intellectual use has evolved significantly.[36] Unlike Schafer, I will take no position on what constitutes a 'good', 'bad' or 'polluted' soundscape. The term is used here more in line with Emily Thompson's interpretation: 'A soundscape is simultaneously

---

[33] See Michael Bull, Les Back and David Howes, eds, *The Auditory Culture Reader* (Bloomsbury Publishing, 2016); Mark Michael Smith, ed., *Hearing History: A Reader* (University of Georgia Press, 2004).

[34] Most famously in Alain Corbin's work on the social rituals and meanings of nineteenth-century French village bells; Alain Corbin, *Village Bells: Sound and Meaning in the Nineteenth Century French Countryside*, trans. Martin Thom (Columbia University Press, 1998).

[35] Sophia Rosenfeld, 'On Being Heard: A Case for Paying Attention to the Historical Ear', *The American Historical Review*, 116:2 (2011), 317.

[36] Ari Y. Kelman, 'Rethinking the Soundscape: A Critical Genealogy of a Key Term in Sound Studies', *The Senses and Society*, 5:2 (2010), 212–34.

a physical environment and a way of perceiving that environment.'[37] The use of 'soundscape' is not uncontroversial. Tim Ingold has gone so far as to write a piece called 'Against Soundscape', which complains that 'the environment that we experience, know and move around is not sliced up along the lines of the sensory pathways by which we enter it'.[38] It is important, then, to clarify that the term is not used here to imply that there is a way of hearing an environment that is separable from other sensory encounters with or aspects of that environment. However, 'soundscape' remains a useful shorthand. It refers simultaneously to the different sounds that – when *perceived*, through feeling and/or hearing – make up the profile of a given space or place, and it brings together the material and social aspects of sound.

This section focuses on the physical environment of the hospital. As Thompson notes, this consists 'not only of the sounds themselves ... but also the material objects that create, and sometimes destroy, those sounds'.[39] The social and cultural aspects of listening are discussed further in the second section, but the 'physical' and the 'social' are divided here only for clarity of analysis. It is important to avoid what Matthew Gandy describes as 'tensions between an emphasis on the spatio-temporal complexities of sound as an acoustic phenomenon and the wider social or historical context within which sound is experienced'.[40] Indeed, no 'soundscape' existed outside of modes of listening and the creation of sonic order. Although this analysis follows a common distinction between the two terms found in geographical literature, in which 'place' is broadly defined as *meaningful* space, it also problematises the division.[41] Hospital sounds and soundscapes were almost always produced, encountered and made meaningful through relationships between people and place. This approach aligns broadly with the theoretical framework outlined by LeFebvre who 'implied that absolute space cannot exist because, at the moment

---

[37] Thompson, *The Soundscape of Modernity*, p. 1; Peter A. Coates, 'The Strange Stillness of the Past: Toward an Environmental History of Sound and Noise', *Environmental History*, 10:4 (2005), 639.

[38] Tim Ingold, 'Against Soundscape' in Angus Caryle, ed. *Autumn Leaves: Sound and the Environment in Artistic Practice* (Double Entendre, 2007), 10. Stefan Helmreich builds on Ingold's work by questioning the concept of 'immersion' implied by 'soundscapes', preferring instead the notion of 'transduction'; see Stefan Helmreich, 'Listening against Soundscapes', *Anthropology News*, 51:9 (2010), 10.

[39] Thompson, *The Soundscape of Modernity*, p. 1.   [40] Gandy, 'Introduction', p. 9.

[41] The analysis distinguishes sounds as part of 'objective' spatiality (floorplans, materials, objects) from sounds experienced as place (affect, atmospheres), see Tim Cresswell, 'Place' in Nigel Thrift and Rob Kitchen, eds, *International Encyclopedia of Human Geography* (Elsevier, 2009), 169–77. These divisions can, though, be problematic. In 'The Spaces of the Hospital: Spatiality and Urban Change in London 1680–1820', *Journal of Architectural Education*, 69:1 (2015), 130–1, Annmarie Adams also rightly notes we should not conflate hospital 'architecture' with 'space'.

it is colonised through social activity it becomes relativised and historicised space'.[42] It also connects with the work of phenomenologists and other scholars who emphasise the importance of embodiment, and embodied practices, in the making of space/place.[43]

In short, this analysis approaches 'sound' as a productive process, rather than a static object of study, which has always been environmental, embodied and social. It identifies some broad changes over time in the acoustic qualities of hospital spaces, but also shows that there was never a static hospital soundscape that simply existed 'out there' to be heard. The same hospital space could sound different over the course of a day, while the soundscape even in a given time and place could vary according to people's sensory sensitivity, health and emotional state.[44] The following analysis first explores different ways of hearing the hospital, and the layers of its soundscapes: surroundings, buildings, people, objects and entertainment. It closes with a discussion of the literature on 'atmospheres', as a way to make some historical sense out of these disorderly cacophonies.[45]

1.1 Hearing History

How can we hear the hubbub of the NHS hospital? There are many limitations to trying to 'hear' a historic hospital due to the embodied and situational nature of listening. A soundscape is always *in* and *of* place, which poses a challenge to historians, as historical locations are impossible to revisit. In a book on the history of hospital interior decoration, it would be conventional to insert images that show the visual qualities of the space and analyse those. Scholars including Elisa Morselli argue that there is also some potential in analysing 'the representation of sonic experience through images'.[46] Photographs of spaces are indeed provided here to evoke ambiance, some of which are drawn from site visits that I made in order to supplement the archive and to listen to a particular environment. However, site visits can tell us only about the built environment and not the other elements of the hospital soundscape; in many cases, the hospital has also evolved through use, wear

---

[42] Phil Hubbard and Rob Kitchin, eds, *Key Thinkers on Space and Place*, 2nd ed. (Sage, 2011), p. 5.

[43] See Tim Ingold and Nigel Thrift, for example, in Hubbard and Kitchin, *Key Thinkers*, p. 7.

[44] Histories of emotions and the senses are interwoven, see Rob Boddice and Mark Smith, *Emotion, Sense, Experience* (Cambridge University Press, 2020).

[45] Discussing spatial theory and 'atmospheric' approaches at the end of the section, rather than outlining them at the start (as is often the convention), allows the hospital's 'messy' acoustic cacophony to be heard; this section seeks to embrace and understand acoustic disorder, before imposing order on its material.

[46] Elisa Morselli, 'Eyes That Hear: The Synesthetic Representation of Soundspace through Architectural Photography', *Ambiances: Environnement sensible, architecture et espace urbain*, 5 (2019), 26.

and tear, and acoustic upgrades. Katherine Fennelly makes similar points in her work on early nineteenth-century asylums, stating that 'recording inside the buildings would not have been useful as modifications, plastering, resurfacing and weathering of the buildings mean that the original effects of noise and light have been altered since construction'.[47] Fennelly chooses to focus on documentary and visual sources, which is a similar approach to that taken here. This analysis also uses some imaginative work, grounded in knowledge of the acoustic qualities of certain spaces and materials, to think about how changes to built environments and materiality might have reshaped its soundscapes.

Narrative analysis provides another valuable route to hearing the hospital cacophony. Oral histories sometimes identify sounds of significance in people's memories of hospital care. Some historical subjects also wrote evocatively on the hospital soundscape, trying to recreate the environment through writing, in a wide range of contexts including medical journals, noise complaints and memoirs. This kind of writing deliberately communicated a specific concern about hospital 'noise', evoking chaos and cacophony. It is not a direct insight into the experience of hospital staff or patients, but such rich descriptions evoke embodied sensations and highlight the subjectivity of listening. A memoir is particularly descriptive and evocative because of its literary form, often replete with metaphor or simile, particularly those with that are written by professional authors. Such texts aid an understanding of how the experience of listening is shaped by sickness and its associated ever-changing mental, physical and emotional aspects.

There are some additional options for historians of the twentieth century. Historians of the NHS can delve into the audiovisual archive, which does open up some interesting possibilities. The BBC sound archives include specific sounds, for example allowing close listening to the nuances of different trolley wheels down a corridor in the 1960s (albeit as 'sound effects' rather than in situ recordings).[48] This kind of listening has informed some of the analysis about the materiality of the trolley and its sounds. Documentaries are also often effective at capturing the historic hospital in action. *It Takes All Sorts* from 1975, for example, was a documentary about Southampton General Hospital's emergency department.[49] The video includes sounds such as emergency alarms and ambulance sirens, alongside more 'mundane'

---

[47] Fennelly, 'Out of Sound, Out of Mind', p. 419.
[48] BBC, 'Trolley Passing in Hospital Corridor – 1966'. To listen to this sound, please follow the link in the References section.
[49] Central Office of Information, *It Takes All Sorts* (1975). This video can be viewed online in order to hear the sounds referenced here, please see the link in the References section.

sounds that were of great importance to the daily routines of staff and patients: hospital radio, the whirring of a floor cleaner at night polishing the corridor floor and the throbbing sound of the hospital laundry in action. As David Theodore argues, fictional videos and documentaries alike were 'staged' and it is important to remember this when using them as sources for sensory history. As with all documentary film, *It Takes All Sorts* must not be viewed simply as an objective account of events; it was produced by the Central Office of Information for the Department of Health and Social Security. However, such videos still allow us to think about why certain sounds were brought to the fore to make positive or negative points about hospital care. Even if all of these sources are understood as part of a genre, Theodore notes, they encourage 'us to start *thinking* about sound by also *listening* to it'.[50] Such videos have informed this analysis in terms of identifying the categories of sound that were important in the making of hospital soundscapes (surroundings, buildings, people, objects and entertainment).

1.2 Surroundings

Hospitals are situated in and surrounded by sound. The exterior soundscape has always been the first sensory encounter on arrival at the hospital. Sounds seep into the hospital through ward windows, and burst in through opening doors. Ambulant patients, staff and visitors move between the internal and external spaces of hospitals, to meet a patient from an arriving ambulance, to take a break on a bench or to have a cigarette. The soundscapes of these thresholds are hugely varied, and this diversity must not be smoothed over in pursuit of an account of 'the' built environment of the NHS hospital and its acoustics.

The sounds outside the hospital depend, first and foremost, on the location of the hospital site. For the city hospital, urbanisation and industrialisation brought new sensory nuisances. There were many geographical distinctions, even within the same country, but modern cities were generally smelly, polluted, busy and noisy. Urbanisation itself brought higher population densities, although suburbanisation reversed this trend somewhat in the late twentieth century. Road travel became more affordable, as living standards rose, meaning that the urban soundscape was populated increasingly by traffic. When 'noise pollution' was discussed in Parliament in relation to the 1960 Noise Abatement Act and in the 1963 report of the Committee on the Problem of Noise, specific vehicular sounds such as motorbikes, train horns and ice cream vans were often highlighted as nuisances.[51] Other new technologies that elicited noise

---

[50] Theodore, 'Sound Medicine'.
[51] Hansard, HC vol. 618, cc1571–632 (4 March 1960); Wilson, *Noise*.

complaints included music systems and loudspeakers. At the same time, 'modernity' – including the 'modern' built environment – came increasingly to represent qualities such as efficiency and control. Modern urban design and architecture sought to eliminate sensory problems, many of which were simultaneously created and tackled by the modern world and its technologies; the hospital was no exception to this paradoxical trend.

The rural hospital was situated in a very different environment, but it would be a mistake to think of the city hospital as 'loud' and the country hospital as 'quiet'. As one article in *The Journal of the Noise Abatement Society* commented in the early 1960s: 'Hospitals situated in town may never be free all day and late into the night from the rumble of heavy traffic, while those in the country, surrounded by lawns and gardens, suffer in the summer from motor-mowers and hedge-cutters.'[52] The external soundscape that surrounded rural and small-town hospitals changed less dramatically than that of the larger urban areas, but they were also not consistent over time. There were subtle alterations to the sound of the natural world, including shifts in weather patterns and changes to biodiversity. Rural areas had growing infrastructure over the late twentieth century, particularly roads and housing. Flight paths grew over some previously quiet areas as local airports expanded. On the other side of this story was the so-called Beeching Axe that closed down over 2,000 small rail stations and over 4,000 miles of track in the 1960s. The steam train, with its distinctive huffing and puffing, made its final passenger journey in the same decade, becoming an option only for heritage passengers. The diesel trains that replaced them were slightly quieter, although complaints about the 'noise' of trains continued – in relation mostly to their horns.[53]

The spatial distribution of hospitals also changed over the course of the late twentieth century. The launch of the NHS aligned broadly with the New Towns Act (1946) that created new population centres, although it would be some time before the hospitals were built to serve them. When the 1962 Hospital Plan finally put into place a large-scale hospital building programme to address shortfalls in provision, there was a fashion for larger district general hospitals (DGHs), many of which were located outside cities for improved accessibility by car or bus. Stevenage, for example, was the first designated 'New Town'. At first, its growing population had to travel around six miles to a small hospital in Hitchin, a building that had previously been a workhouse. A larger DGH (the Lister) was developed and built over the course of the 1960s and finally opened

---

[52] An Assistant Matron, 'Noise in Hospitals', *QP: The Journal of the Noise Abatement Society*, 1:2 (1961), 11.

[53] Wellcome Library, London, 'Records of the Noise Abatement Society', SA/NAS (uncatalogued), accession number 2131, Boxes 20–22.

in 1972, two miles from the town centre and a railway station that would open the following year.[54]

The sounds that surrounded such hospitals were inevitably different from those of the conventional city-centre hospital, the small rural hospital or even the market-town cottage hospital that Stevenage's population had previously used. There was significant traffic, but typically from patients, visitors, ambulances and other hospital transport, rather than the background of urban activity heard in city-centre premises. Such traffic sounds also increased over time, in quality as well as quantity. Ambulance sirens gradually replaced bells in the 1960s, for example, and audiovisual archives indicate that the infamous 'nee naw' sound of the 1970s ambulance differed significantly from the trilling sound of ambulance bells of the 1950s.[55] As one hospital employee noted in the 1980s, the 'siren-shrieking ambulance in full cry' soon became a key and highly emotive part of the A&E (accident and emergency department) soundscape.[56] Its significance is also demonstrated within popular culture, including the centrality of the ambulance – and its sounds – to the opening credits of the BBC television show *Casualty* (1986–present).

New hospitals on the urban fringe often gave extensive space to car parks, but many also built green space into their immediate surroundings. The Royal Bournemouth Hospital, for example, opened its first phase in 1989 and had a landscaped lake between staff residences and the hospital. As Figure 1 shows, a lake of this kind encouraged the presence of wildlife and offered resting places for patients, visitors or staff as a reprieve from the hospital's interior soundscape. Hospital gardens had a long history of offering such sensory respite, but such environments also took on specific significance in relation to the modern hospital. The sounds of 'nature', particularly in open spaces that felt more 'wild' than landscaped courtyards, came to represent the opposite of (and implicit counterbalance to) high-technology environments.

1.3 Buildings

There was also no such thing as 'the' NHS hospital, even at a given point in time. There is no simple story to tell of the rise of modern hospital buildings

---

[54] This time frame was fairly typical, see Sarah Hosking and Liz Haggard, *Healing the Hospital Environment: Design, Management and Maintenance of Healthcare Premises* (E & FN Spon, 1999), p. 14.

[55] Audiovisual materials allow us to hear this difference; compare, for example, Central Office of Information, *It Takes All Sorts* with British Pathé, 'Premature Baby Unit 1950'. Again, links to listen to this material online are available in the References section.

[56] Julian Ashley, *Anatomy of a Hospital* (Oxford University Press, 1987), p. 39.

Figure 1 Royal Bournemouth Hospital, opened in 1989, photographed in 2019. © The author. Printed with permission of University Hospitals Dorset NHS Foundation Trust.

marked by quiet efficiency. The service inherited over 2,000 hospitals that had previously been looked after by a combination of county authorities, municipal authorities and voluntary organisations.[57] These built environments created complex soundscapes: old buildings accommodated new technologies, new medical practices, a higher number and turnover of patients, a growing emphasis on efficient working, and the welfare state's democratic principles of care. The NHS also never truly succeeded in standardising hospital design. Even when new hospitals were built, older ones were not simply abandoned and many stayed in use. These buildings were not passive structures within which sounds were produced. Built environments – including their shape, substance and surroundings – were material agents in making hospital soundscapes. A heterogeneous combination of layouts and materials continuously (re)shaped the hospital soundscape over the years of the NHS.

There were some common trends in early hospitals that had implications for the hospital soundscape. Perhaps the most famous – and enduring – part of inherited hospitals was the open Victorian 'Nightingale ward' (Figure 2). Open wards were designed with light, fresh air and cross-ventilation in mind. This design was linked to the contemporary miasma theory of disease, and the layout assisted nurses with the monitoring of patients. The layout also meant that these wards were busy and sound travelled easily. Nightingale had been concerned about patients' experiences in such spaces, with her aforementioned comments about 'noise' as an 'absence of care' sitting alongside other points on the importance of making wards homely and comfortable.

Recent studies of sites in which such wards still exist have found that open-plan wards are perceived as 'significantly noisier' than the bay wards that replaced them.[58] One surgeon who worked in St Bart's Hospital in the post-war years also observed, in an oral history interview, that: 'On the ward rounds of course you stand round the bed and of course it was a Nightingale ward . . . so the curtains of course don't cut out the sound . . . all the other patients on the ward would be able to hear exactly what was going on.'[59] Sound could not easily be controlled or managed in such spaces; as Tom Rice has recently noted about open-plan wards, there is a constant 'leakage or seepage' of bodily sounds, conversation and 'sonically coded' medical information.[60]

---

[57] Glanville, Noble, and Scher, *50 Years*, p. 15.
[58] Helen M. Pattison and Claire E. Robertson, 'The Effect of Ward Design on the Well-being of Post-operative Patients', *Journal of Advanced Nursing*, 23:4 (1996), 820.
[59] NHS at 70, Edmund Hoare interview, NHSat70_EdmundHoare_03072018.
[60] Tom Rice, *Hearing the Hospital: Sound, Listening, Knowledge and Experience* (Sean Kingston Press, 2013), p. 45.

A CONTRAST: THE "FLORENCE NIGHTINGALE" WARD IN ST. THOMAS'S HOSPITAL, WESTMINSTER
Miss Florence Nightingale, who was born at Florence on May 12th, 1820, is a Lady of Grace of St. John of Jerusalem

Figure 2 St Thomas' Hospital: 'Florence Nightingale' ward. Photogravure
after A. Rischgitz. Wellcome Collection.

Nightingale wards fell out of fashion in new NHS buildings, due to problems related both to peace and privacy. In 1949, a multidisciplinary team led by the architect Richard Llewelyn-Davies began a project for the Nuffield Provincial Hospitals Trust, a health charity, to study and improve hospitals that the NHS had inherited.[61] These studies were later published as *Studies in the Function and Design of Hospitals* (1955) and recommended ways of making new hospitals more efficient, including bays instead of open-plan wards.[62] However, early attempts to implement the Nuffield recommendations were hampered by resources. Hospital development in the 1950s tended to take the form of upgrades rather than new buildings. Some of these renovations involved reorganising floor plans or even rebuilding entire departments, but many others were smaller scale such as the upgrading of interior design, technologies, systems and/or materials. The Nuffield study itself recognised that it might not always be possible to implement 'best practice' in existing hospitals and gave advice for improving existing spaces; as Section 2 shows, these recommendations included upgrading acoustic materials on wards. This renovation trend continued alongside new-build sites, discussed later, many of which supplemented rather than replaced existing hospitals. As late as 2012, more than one-fifth of NHS acute hospitals pre-dated 1948, some of which were still

---

[61] On the team's research methods see Theodore, 'Treating Architectural Research'.
[62] Nuffield Provincial Hospitals Trust, *Studies in the Functions and Design of Hospitals*.

dominated by Nightingale wards.[63] Upgrades to acoustic materials could not entirely eliminate the sounds of such communal, busy spaces.

Under the eventual impetus of the Hospital Plan, some hospitals were replaced or supplemented by new large DGHs or teaching hospitals over the course of the subsequent decade. The largest hospitals were built from scratch, while others were expanded with new blocks. There was little standardisation of design at this point, but there was a general tendency to meet the expanded needs of the NHS by building upwards, as had been the trend in large schemes throughout the post-war period.[64] Examples include Hull Royal Infirmary, completed in 1967 as a fourteen-storey building, the fifteen-storey Charing Cross General Teaching Hospital (Figure 3), which opened in 1973, and the Royal Hallamshire Hospital in Sheffield, opened over the course of the 1970s with a mammoth twenty storeys above ground.

These buildings took forwards a vision of the new 'modern' NHS through larger, flexible, functional buildings that would allow for new technologies and changing treatment practices.[65] However, many of these new buildings used materials that were less absorbent than traditional brick structures. As Annmarie Adams notes, in relation to early twentieth-century Canada, the emphasis on noise control in such spaces was ironic because 'it was modern construction and planning that created these noise problems in the hospital'.[66] David Theodore similarly describes the balance between terrazzo floor coverings, stainless fittings and acoustic ceiling tiles in hospital corridors as 'an architecture that simultaneously produces unwanted sounds and tries to mitigate them'.[67] It should not be assumed that new buildings meant quieter buildings.

Taking building ventilation as an example, it is possible to see (or hear) the limitations of thinking about hospital soundscapes purely in terms of 'less' or 'more'. New buildings were increasingly sealed systems, which often resulted in less external sound from the street and fewer banging windows but more internal sound in order to maintain environmental controls. In the 1960s, it was common to find complaints about 'windows rattling in the wind' in hospitals.[68] This kind of sound was not consistent; it was partly the result of building design, which allowed for windows to be opened, but only occurred in specific weather conditions that differed across time and place. It was then largely eliminated as

[63] Kevin J. Lomas, Renganathan Giridharan, C. Alan Short and A. J. Fair, 'Resilience of "Nightingale" Hospital Wards in a Changing Climate', *Building Services Engineering Research and Technology*, 33:1 (2012), 81.
[64] Hughes, 'Matchbox on a Muffin', p. 41.   [65] Hughes, 'Matchbox on a Muffin', p. 33.
[66] Adams, *Medicine by Design*, pp. 112–13.   [67] Theodore, 'Sound Medicine', p. 993.
[68] An Assistant Matron, 'Noise', p. 11.

Figure 3 Charing Cross Hospital. Hammersmith, London: under construction, 1972. Photograph by H. Windsley. Wellcome Collection.

a sound in many new NHS hospitals, where the opening of windows was not possible. There was continued belief in the health benefits of ventilation, even after the decline of miasma theory and rise of germ theory at the turn of the century, but it was increasingly common for fresh air to be replaced with other systems. Jeanne S. Kisacky's work, on the USA, shows that the rise of antibiotics and aseptic practices meant that it was 'believed that patient healthiness could be maintained regardless of room design ... Windows were no longer necessary to healthy hospitals.'[69] The growing interest in environmental control and 'efficiency' in NHS hospitals, including energy efficiency, fuelled the trend. Higher buildings also meant that sealed windows were preferred for safety reasons. By the 1970s, some spaces requiring atmospheric control were entirely

---

[69] Jeanne Kisacky, 'When Fresh Air Went Out of Fashion at Hospitals', *Smithsonian Magazine*, 14 June 2017, www.smithsonianmag.com/history/when-fresh-air-went-out-fashion-hospitals -180963710/ (accessed: 8 January 2021).

mechanically ventilated; for example, *Hospital Development* (*HD*) reported in 1976 on a new 'Special Baby Care Unit where the nurseries are fully air conditioned to the required level of temperature and humidity. All nurseries are fully glazed', and in 1985, on a patient isolation unit which was 'air conditioned, maintaining a constant 20°C and the humidity can be varied to meet the specific needs of the patient'.[70]

Air-conditioned blocks cut out external sounds from the street, but added those of the air-conditioning units. Even 'quiet' ones contributed to changes in hospital acoustics, especially when combined with other developments in building materials. Sinéad Gleeson has recently written eloquently on the sound of hospital air conditioning in her book *Constellations: Reflections from Life* (2019). She notes that, having not even noticed the air conditioning for weeks, 'it appears like tinnitus, and the rattle becomes an anti-earworm ... it thunders through every night'.[71] The 'rattle' of the window has thus been replaced by the 'rattle' of the air-conditioning unit, though the same descriptive term does not denote the *same sound*. Gleeson's work implicitly refers to her experiences in Irish hospitals, but its significance extends to the contexts described here. This quote is a reminder of the importance of perception and of the relationship between sound and listener. Not only might the same sound have been heard differently by two people in the same room, for a wide range of reasons ranging from hearing ability to emotional state, but the same person might hear the same hospital room differently over time. As Margo Annemans *et al.* have recently argued, '[a]t a different moment of the day, what someone sees, hears, or smells can be experienced completely differently, although it may be the same scene, number of decibels, or odor'.[72] The sound of the air conditioning might be significant because it is very unusual for people to have air conditioning in British homes, making it unfamiliar, and it is a sound over which patients have never been given control. Air-conditioning units have been developed to be less 'loud' in the traditional sense, but they still 'rattle', and what is quiet to one person might be 'thunder' to another when trying to sleep.

Each new building type added acoustic challenges while solving others. By 1974, to quote a later *HD* article, it was clear that there were 'design mistakes' in the DGHs, including problems of 'temperature, lighting levels

---

[70] Anon., 'Royal Lancaster Infirmary Maternity Unit', *Hospital Development*, 4:6 (1976), 24; Anon., 'Patient Isolation Unit from MDH', *Hospital Development*, 13:4 (1985), 19.

[71] Sinéad Gleeson, *Constellations: Reflections from Life* (Picador, 2019), p. 109.

[72] Margo Annemans, Chantal van Audenhove, Hilde Vermolen and Ann Heylighen, 'Inpatients' Spatial Experience: Interactions between Material, Social, and Time-Related Aspects', *Space and Culture*, 21:4 (2018), 505.

and noise'.[73] At the time there were a few rare, but important, examples of lower-rise design, such as Wexham Park in Slough and Greenwich District Hospital in London. Lower-level wards returned patients to close proximity with the sounds of the street, the natural world or perhaps the hospital entrance and car park, depending on where the hospital was located, which direction the ward faced and whether the building had windows that could open. There was a return to the use of courtyards, which had otherwise been abandoned in new hospital planning: Wexham Park, for example, had twenty internal brick, grass or landscaped courts, ranging from 136 × 40 ft (~41.5 × 12 m) to 20 ft square (~1.9 m²); Greenwich had two courts of 64 ft square (~6 m²) and one 64 × 32 ft (~19.5 × 9.8 m) on its ground floor, planted with trees, although the windows were 'for daylighting only' and did not open onto the outdoor spaces.[74] Even where inaudible from wards, these kind of external spaces were easily accessible from multiple points in the hospital and offered their own soundscape for patients and staff to seek out. They often provided relative peace and quiet compared with the busy hospital, as well as new sounds where biodiversity was encouraged or fountains installed.

The trend for low- and medium-rise hospitals of this kind soon gathered pace, as discontent with the high-rise DGHs became more widespread. When Queen Alexandra Hospital in Portsmouth was expanded in the early 1970s, its ward blocks were built to be only five storeys high and it used a 'central hospital "street"' for the purposes of 'traffic circulation'.[75] In the mid 1970s, a financial crisis meant that the hospital building programme was halted, and when it was started again, there was even more focus on these lower-level buildings and more standardised hospital designs. All new hospitals had to give consideration to using the standardised nucleus form, which involved a cruciform 'template' of 1,000 m² (which could be expanded with further 'templates' when required). These nucleus hospitals started to be built in the early 1980s, with over 130 built in due course.[76] They followed the model of a village or small town, which meant that sound was further redistributed along horizontal rather than vertical lines. Many of these hospitals also included energy efficiency measures, which often brought improvement both to the thermal and acoustic absorption/insulation properties of a building.[77]

---

[73] Anon., 'Viewpoint', *Hospital Development*, 12:9 (1984), 12.

[74] William A. Guttridge, 'Courtyards in Hospital Planning', *Hospital Development*, 2:5 (1974), 34.

[75] Brenda Inglis, 'Wessex', *Hospital Development*, 1:6 (1973), 30.

[76] Glanville, Noble, and Scher, *50 Years*, p. 37.

[77] See, for example, the energy-efficient nucleus St Mary's Hospital on the Isle of Wight, completed in 1990; Richard Burton, 'St Mary's Hospital', *British Medical Journal*, 301:6766 (1990), 1424.

This shift towards horizontal routes through the hospital, with more time spent in corridors and less time in lifts, changed the ways that people moved through, made sound in and heard the hospital. These design choices removed some of the sounds associated with the materiality and layout of high-rise buildings such as lifts and reverberation, while (re)introducing others. Large hospitals with lower, wider layouts often required lengthy pipework for plumbing, heating and communications. The scale of these systems brought banging, gurgling, whooshing and the occasional passage of a pneumatic tube. Taking York Hospital as an example, the hospital opened in stages in 1976–7, with over 800 beds, thirty wards and four-storey-high ward blocks with a long corridor or 'main street' to connect services.[78] Figure 4 shows one of the hospital's streets, situated 'behind the scenes'.

These long corridors of hospital infrastructure, through which estate staff navigated the hospital, were very different from the hospital highways taken by other staff members, patients and visitors. A member of staff moving through the main hospital corridor would have heard trolleys, shoes and conversation, punctuated by sporadic sounds from open doorways as they passed. Walking the 'corridors' of Figure 4, in contrast, would mean encountering a soundscape dominated by infrastructure and the flow of resources around the hospital building. The difference between the soundscapes of these different areas is qualitative; it cannot be reduced to 'more' or 'less' sound, or the presence or absence of 'noise'.

In the final decades of the century, hospital design trends changed once more and new architectural features changed their acoustics yet further. The atrium became an increasingly common feature of new-build and renovated NHS hospitals alike from the late 1980s onwards and were particularly common in paediatric hospitals internationally. Atriums are often the full height of a building and use extensive glass, housing waiting areas alongside high-street shops and cafés. They have careful acoustic design, but even acoustic insulation and absorption cannot entirely mitigate the inherently reverberant acoustics of large spaces in which sounds tend to travel and intermingle.[79] In Britain, the popularity of such spaces related to the rise of the patient-consumer, and to efforts to 'humanise' hospitals by evoking non-clinical buildings to make them feel less cold.[80] The acoustics of this kind of environment were novel and

---

[78] Katherine A. Webb, *From County Hospital to NHS Trust: The History and Archives of NHS Hospitals, Services and Management in York, 1740–2000* (Borthwick Publications, 2002), p. 175.

[79] Bing Chen and Jian Kang, 'Acoustic Comfort in Shopping Mall Atrium Spaces: A Case Study in Sheffield Meadowhall', *Architectural Science Review*, 47:2 (2004), 107–14.a

[80] On the rise of the 'patient-consumer', see Alex Mold, 'Patient Groups and the Construction of the Patient-Consumer in Britain: An Historical Overview', *Journal of Social Policy*, 39:4 (2010), 505–21.

Figure 4 York Hospital, opened in 1976–7, photographed in 2020. © The author. Printed with permission of York Teaching Hospital NHS Foundation Trust.

Figure 5 Southmead Hospital Brunel building atrium at night, opened in 2014, photographed in 2019. © The author. Printed with permission of North Bristol NHS Trust.

often evoked a different kind of space entirely. At night or in quiet times, the hospital atrium also has the very specific acoustic quality of large, empty spaces, a quality more commonly discussed in relation to religious spaces such as churches (see Figure 5).[81]

In busy times, atrium acoustics contributed to an atmosphere similar to that of a shopping centre, airport or – in the words of Annmarie Adams and David Theodore – a 'mundane shopping mall'.[82] In Britain, it might also be no coincidence that atriums that evoked non-medical sites, such as shopping centres or airports, were increasingly popular with the rise of the public finance

---

[81] See Beth Williamson, 'Sensory Experience in Medieval Devotion: Sound and Vision, Invisibility and Silence', *Speculum*, 88:1 (2013), 1–43.

[82] Annmarie Adams and David Theodore, 'The Architecture of Children's Hospitals in Toronto and Montreal, 1875–2010', in Cheryl Krasnick Warsh and Veronica Strong-Boag, eds, *Children's Health Issues in Historical Perspective* (Wilfrid Laurier University Press, 2005), p. 466.

initiative (PFI) hospital at the end of the century. As Gesler *et al.* note, PFI design had a number of goals, including commercial ones: 'while old hospitals are depicted as institutional, uncomfortable, and "public": – in the negative sense of an absence-of-privacy for patients or staff – new hospitals are compared favourably with privately owned commercial buildings such as hotels, offices, and supermarkets'.[83] PFI brought together construction with design, and closed the gap between public and private sectors, to a degree unprecedented in the NHS.

Many of the changes outlined here could be seen as international stories, but NHS architecture also related to specific principles of the welfare state. There was collaboration between private architects and those employed by the state, to a degree not found in many other countries. Post-war hospital building aligned with other kinds of public building programmes such as schools, and with other post-war community health buildings as part of public planning, such as leisure centres. The NHS also had a unique set of challenges, in terms of the infrastructure that it inherited and the sheer extent of what it needed to build. Its specific mixture of old and new architecture and design disrupts narratives about the 'new' noises of mid-to-late twentieth-century Britain.

1.4 People

Hospital soundscapes have always been dominated by people. The new NHS offered healthcare free at the point of delivery, which increased demand for British hospitals significantly. This demand was also fuelled by medical advances, including the availability of new surgical procedures, and a growing population. Reports of the Ministry of Health for England and Wales showed that between 1949 and 1953 alone, the number of inpatients rose from 2.9 million to 3.5 million, the number of new outpatients (per year) rose from 6.1 million to 6.7 million, and the number of full-time medical and dental staff, nurses and midwives rose from 134,706 to 155,299.[84] By 1977, there were a record 5.35 million inpatients, 7.61 million outpatients, and 8.9 million accident and emergency cases treated during the year.[85] Inpatient stays were also getting shorter, and the number of beds was dropping. Overall, then, the picture of the NHS hospital is one that was getting not only busier, in

---

[83] Wil Gesler, Morag Bell, Sarah Curtis, Phil Hubbard and Susan Francis, 'Therapy by Design: Evaluating the UK Hospital Building Program', *Health & Place*, 10:2 (2004), 123.

[84] Ministry of Health, *Report for the Year Ended 31st December 1953: Part I* (HM Stationery Office, 1954), appendix 2.

[85] Department of Health and Social Security (DHSS), *Annual Report 1977* (HM Stationery Office, 1978), p. 28.

terms of patients and staff alike, but in which each patient was moving through the hospital at a more rapid pace.

The nature of the population visiting and working in hospitals also shifted. As the government turned towards 'care in the community' and sought to end long-term inpatient stays for specific types of patient – such as 'geriatric' and 'psychiatric' patients, to use the terminology of the time – there was a significant rise in the number of such patients attending hospitals as 'regular day patients'.[86] There were also changes to the general British population, including more movement both within and beyond national borders, leading to a wider range of languages and accents being heard within the hospital walls. In particular, the NHS was highly dependent on the recruitment of international staff to meet growing demands on the service. The launch of the NHS actually broadly aligned with the 1948 British Nationality Act, which gave citizenship to Commonwealth citizens. Hospitals had an increasingly global workforce in the late twentieth century, and by 1971, almost a third of English NHS doctors were born and qualified overseas.[87] These factors reshaped the hospital soundscape in subtle ways.

Visiting hours changed significantly over the course of the late twentieth century. They had previously been extremely limited, with visiting cards and, in some hospitals, a restriction to adult visitors only. One of the most significant changes to visiting rules came after 1959, when the Platt report made a case for 'open' visiting to children's wards, for the sake of their emotional health. There was no overnight change to visiting hours, but this report did start an attitude change and the gradual – albeit uneven – expansion of visiting hours for adults and children alike. In an article on the history of hospital visiting times, Sadia Ismail and Graham Mulley note that 'in the 1980s and 1990s many hospitals started restricted visiting again' because of concerns about the impact of open visiting hours on patient care and confidentiality.[88] Despite these restrictions and regional variations, it is reasonable to conclude that visitors were in hospitals at a wider range of times – and for longer – at the end of the century than when the NHS was launched. The concentrated chatter that came with very restricted visiting hours, especially when hospitals had larger wards, was gradually phased out. This changing pattern meant that there was a greater likelihood of people having their visitors at different times. Humans were also

---

[86] DHSS, *Annual Report 1977*, p. 28.

[87] Stephanie Snow and Emma Jones, 'Immigration and the National Health Service: Putting History to the Forefront', *History and Policy* (2011), www.historyandpolicy.org/policy-papers/papers/immigration-and-the-national-health-service-putting-history-to-the-forefron (accessed: 6 January 2021).

[88] Sadia Ismail and Graham Mulley, 'Visiting Times', *British Medical Journal*, 335:7633 (2007), 1317.

not the only living creatures who visited hospitals. Sound-making animals often moved through as both uninvited guests (such as urban rats, or birds coming in through windows), as service and companion animals, and – albeit in an increasingly controlled way – as part of the long history of therapeutic animal use (or 'animal assisted interventions').[89] As Steven Connor notes in relation to urban birdsong, the contributions such creatures might make to soundscapes were varied: 'frequency, amplitude, phrasing, syntax, patterning, redundancy'.[90]

People – and animals – moved through the hospital in very specific ways, and with particular temporalities, depending on their purpose. Outpatients popped in for tests in some areas, while long-term inpatients rested in others; the slow-moving or immobile sick recuperated in wards, while hospital staff moved rapidly around them, barely pausing for a cup of tea; people gave birth slowly and people died quickly, and *vice versa*; people paced anxiously and waited excitedly for news. Many of these ways of moving have stayed consistent over time, but there were also some changes to the spatiality of NHS hospital care, for example, in consequence of the refinement of systems such as triage and progressive patient care.[91] Progressive patient care grew in popularity from the 1960s onwards, as a way to continue to provide high-quality care without escalating costs, and it had implications for the spatial distribution of sound. Progressive patient care meant that patients were organised by nursing and medical needs, rather than grouped in wards by illness category as had been traditional. They were moved – or progressed – towards discharge in what critics described as something of an 'assembly line'.[92] In 1973, *HD* reported on the implications of progressive patient care: 'the noise factor is introduced when [high dependency] beds are located beside the ward entrance. This has been overcome by siting the high dependency beds opposite the entrance to the ward complex but connected to it by a short corridor.'[93] Progressive patient care created new 'noise factors', which – in turn – necessitated spatial reorganisation

---

[89] Julie M. MacDonald and David Barrett, 'Companion Animals and Well-being in Palliative Care Nursing: A Literature Review', *Journal of Clinical Nursing*, 25:3–4 (2016), 300–10; Hospital Senses Collective, 'Wards' (online booklet forthcoming at https://hospitalsenses.co.uk); Isobel Toy, 'Pawprints in the Hospital', Society for the Social History of Medicine blogs, https://sshm.org/undergraduate-essay-prize-blogs/pawprints-in-the-hospital/ (accessed: 8 January 2021).

[90] Steven Connor, 'Rustications: Animals in the Urban Mix', in Matthew Gandy and B. J. Nilsen, eds, *The Acoustic City* (Jovis, 2014), p. 20.

[91] On the history of triage and its spatiality, see Graham Mooney, 'From Casualty Room to A&E', www.rcpe.ac.uk/heritage/talks/casualty-room-ae-history-hospital-space (accessed: 8 January 2021).

[92] Anon., 'Progressive Patient Care', *British Medical Journal*, 1:1816 (1962), 1816–17.

[93] Inglis, 'Wessex', p. 26.

to resolve them. The positioning of 'high dependency beds' away from other patients and down 'a short corridor' also indicates a growing interest in the aural needs of patients, which were prioritised in this example over the convenience of staff.

Other changes were inextricably woven with changes to the built environment, which created new ways of moving, interacting and waiting; all of these, in turn, changed hospital soundscapes. Rivett, for example, notes that the lifts necessary for high-rise hospitals 'affected the way staff met and talked. People did not meet each other as they did in, for example, the St Thomas' long corridor.'[94] Conversations between staff still happened, of course, but their spatiality changed. Lifts created the illusion of contained acoustic space and created new problems of breaches of privacy, to the extent that a number of NHS hospitals put up signs to remind staff to avoid 'inappropriate talk in lifts'.[95] The decline of the Nightingale wards also created new movement patterns for staff, with patient privacy coming at the cost of ease of observation: staff had to spend more time moving in and out of bays, creating a different spatiality to the hospital soundscape that followed their movement patterns. The 1955 Nuffield publication (Figure 6) showed that the hospital floorplan changed how nurses moved through corridors and wards by comparing a Nightingale ward with smaller bays. The design of hospital spaces did not entirely determine behaviours of course; there were also accounts of nurses moving patients at night into corridors to aid observation, rather than providing care in precisely the ways that the space demanded.[96] However, evolving hospital designs and medical practices had implications for the ways in which people moved through and made sound in the built environment.

The lines in Figure 6 can be reinterpreted as the depiction of sound, as created through the movement of people. They visually represent how the Nightingale ward put patients in the centre of an almost continual flurry of movement, and how the shift away from these wards led to nurses spending a lot more time in corridors. They also demonstrate the many different sound-producing spaces in which nurses spent time, such as the hospital kitchen with its clattering pans and the sluice room with its banging bin lids. There were, of course, also times of day in which movement around the hospital was much more limited. As one recently retired nurse reminisced in an interview for the 'NHS at 70' project, 'I always liked the hospital corridor

---

[94] Geoffrey Rivett, *From Cradle to Grave: Fifty Years of the NHS* (King's Fund, 1998), p. 263.

[95] Douglas Carnall, 'Hospitals Warn against Stories between Storeys', *British Medical Journal*, 311:7004 (1995), 528.

[96] Rivett, *From Cradle to Grave*, p. 263.

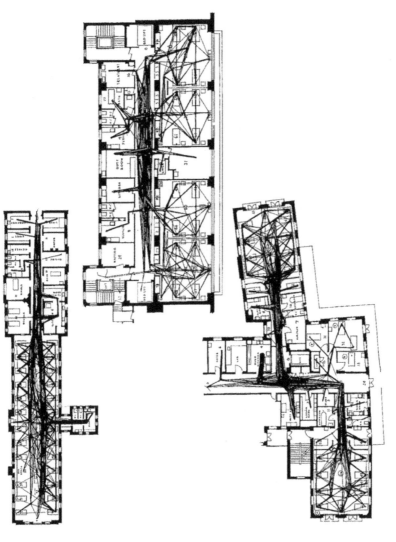

Figure 6 Nurse movement studies, 1955. © The Nuffield Trust. Reproduced with permission of the Nuffield Trust. [97]

---

[97] Nuffield Provincial Hospitals Trust, *Studies in the Functions and Design of Hospitals*, p. 9.

at night when it was quiet ... it just felt quite secure'.[98] Such interviews provide insights into sensory memory, the temporality of movement and the changing *feel* of hospital acoustics in specific spaces.

The discussion of 'people' to this point has perhaps implied that sound-making was an inevitable consequence of their presence in the hospital, as the result of necessary activity such as movement, talking during visits or the expression of pain. It is also, though, important to recognise – in Megan Graham's words – that the production of sound is also a 'shared embodied social practice with cultural meaning and embedded in webs of social relationships'.[99] Graham shows this through ethnographic work in a long-term care facility for people living with dementia, emphasising that acoustic practices could be used to 'constitute self-hood, establish intersubjective relationship and resist institutional power'.[100] People produced sounds for a range of reasons, including the expression of agency or as part of social relations. People also never just 'made' or 'received' sound. Bodies changed the acoustic quality of spaces, for example, by absorbing reverberant sound. Patients were not simply passive recipients of the hospital soundscape but an active – and meaningful – part of its production.

1.5 Objects

The hospital soundscape was constantly being remade through interactions between people and objects. Hospitals have always been sites of routine and structure, which produce specific sounds at particular times of day, starting with what Tom Rice identifies as the 'hospital dawn chorus'.[101] In the early 1960s, for example, a report from Guy's Hospital showed that the breakfast trolley arrived at 6.15 am.[102] The maintenance and cleaning of new floors often involved the movement of loud floor polishers at specific times, providing a source of complaints when they conflicted with patients' rest. These elements of routine were supplemented by a range of more chaotic or continuous sounds, also associated with movement of objects. In *QP: The Journal of the Noise Abatement Society* in 1961, one 'assistant matron' wrote evocatively of the constant sounds of hospital activity, including:

> [b]edpans crashing in sluices and dishes in kitchens; metal screens or curtains on rails rattling; chairs, beds and bedtables scraping on floors; electric polishers whining and thudding into beds; windows rattling in the wind;

---

[98] NHS at 70, Shirley Herdman interview, NHSat70_ShirleyHerdman_02092019.

[99] Megan E. Graham, 'Re-socialising Sound: Investigating Sound, Selfhood and Intersubjectivity among People Living with Dementia in Long-Term Care', *Sound Studies*, 5:2 (2019), 176.

[100] Graham, 'Re-socialising Sound', p. 187.   [101] Rice, *Hearing the Hospital*, p. 34.

[102] London Metropolitan Archives (LMA), 'Evaluation of New Guy's House – Draft Documents and Circulars to Working Party', A/KE/I/01/24/060.

food wagons and laundry trolleys thundering along the corridors; the ever-ringing telephone.[103]

This article offers a rare insight into how one staff member engaged with and heard the sounds of the hospital. It emphasises the sensory embodiment of being a hospital worker at the centre of a whirlwind of activity ('crashing ... rattling ... thundering'). This writing shows the value of thinking about hospital sounds in qualitative terms, rather than just as lists of 'noises', and the importance of descriptive language. In this example, the '-ing' form emphasises the motion of objects and brings sound into being as a process, rather than a static object of study. Language also has an aesthetic quality here as onomatopoeia: the heavy sound of 'thud' communicates the feel of sounds through the literary form.

As emerging literatures on the materialities of care have shown, objects in healthcare settings are not just passive recipients of human touch and motion; they are an active force in the making of hospital soundscapes.[104] The materiality of any hospital object shaped its acoustic and reverberant qualities, which could change – in the absence of human intervention – in response to factors ranging from age to temperature. Taking hospital dressing trolleys as a case study, the Science Museum holds examples from 1970 to 1974, depicted in Figure 7.

These trolleys were used in a range of contexts, including wards and operating theatres, to hold instruments and dressings. Their small, hard rolling wheels created a low rumbling sound, differing from the softer rotation of bigger and rubber-based wheels such as those on a wheelchair. Small wheels of this kind got dirty and stiff, and squeaks or creaks emerged over time if wheels were not oiled. The movement away from soft furnishings such as carpets in hospitals towards hard, more hygienic and wipeable flooring made them more audible. These trolley wheels creaking, rumbling, trundling or – to repeat words quoted earlier – thundering along corridors brought sound into being as a material entity, felt through vibrations and motion. Once in use, the materiality of the trolleys also shaped the sounds produced. Here, the two trolleys in Figure 7 differ. The example on the left is made of glass and steel; putting metal equipment down on glass would have produced a high, clean contact sound. The plastic swab bowl, on the right, was comparatively soft and muffled. Indeed, the rise of plastic hospital equipment was a significant and often overlooked part of the history of NHS hospital sound, as the plastics industry expanded significantly after the Second World War. As one article in *The Lancet* observed, in relation to an intensive care

---

[103] An Assistant Matron, 'Noise', p. 11.

[104] See, for example, Christina Buse, Daryl Martin and Sarah Nettleton, eds, *Materialities of Care: Encountering Health and Illness through Artefacts and Architecture* (Wiley Blackwell, 2018).

Figure 7 Square hospital dressing trolley, England, 1970–4, and hospital dressing trolley, England, 1970–4. © Science Museum/Science & Society Picture Library. Reproduced with permission of the Science & Society Picture Library.

ward in the mid 1960s, 'the use of polypropylene equipment' was an important contributor to a sense of 'peace' reported by patients, even when there was no 'lack of activity in the ward'.[105] Such materials were used at first for their durability and hygienic properties but, as noted later, soon became part of deliberate design strategies to combat hospital 'noise'.

The material qualities of the trolley, alongside other factors such as wear and tear, meant that some staff members or long-stay patients could distinguish the sounds of different trolleys moving around. Such subtle differences in acoustic qualities are more important than they might seem. The sound of the trolley might signify very different things, from medical treatment to tea. As Shanti Sumartojo and Sarah Pink show in their study of an older persons' psychiatric inpatient unit, 'trolleys . . . had to be present in order for atmospheres of care to coalesce . . . because the patients in that ward were themselves less able to move around'.[106] In some spaces, the trolley could be a source of noise complaint, as

---

[105] F. Ronald Edwards, J. C. Richardson and P. M. Ashworth, 'Experience with an Intensive-Care Ward', *The Lancet*, 285:7390 (1965), 856.

[106] Shanti Sumartojo and Sarah Pink, *Atmospheres and the Experiential World: Theory and Methods* (Routledge, 2018), p. 83.

Section 2 shows, while in others, the squeaky trundle of its wheels down a corridor bringing food or laundry could help to produce an atmosphere of care for patients. It could also bring a sense of well-being for staff delivering that care, who might be members of staff often overlooked in traditional narratives of the NHS, such as catering or laundry staff.

The hospital trolley is given here as an example of a low-technology object that made sound because of its materiality, use and/or a lack of maintenance. Other sound-producing objects involved with medical care were *designed* to be louder, or at least were innately loud because of motorised and electrical elements. Surgery, for example, often involved cutting-edge motorised technologies in a sterile, acoustically reverberant environment, as well as the more familiar sounds of surgeons chatting and listening to music.[107] It might be easy to categorise such spaces as simply 'noisy', but they merit closer listening. The patient's perspective warns against assuming that sensory experiences of surgical spaces – or the equipment associated with surgery, upon awakening – were inherently bad. Within the British Library collection 'Interviews with Deafened People', for example, one interviewee born in 1948 spoke about going to an English hospital aged eleven for 'hole in the heart surgery': 'I remember being in an oxygen tent … there was … like an elephant's trunk at the back of me which was just wafting in this oxygen from time to time, so there was a noise of like a sea breeze coming in. And I just thought it was a wonderful experience.'[108] The 'sea breeze' sound is actually a positive 'noise' in this account, with strong cultural associations with non-clinical environments and relaxation. This interview also shows that listening and hearing were embodied rather than purely aural experiences, particularly when sounds were rhythmic, reverberant, affective and/or combined with other sensory experiences.[109] It is also significant that this interviewee later had hearing loss, meaning that memories of sound might have taken on particular significance. Sensory experiences of hospitals were given meaning in relation to people's life histories.

The intensive care unit (ICU) provides another example of a high-technology space, often cited in relation to the problem of 'noise' because of its monitoring

---

[107] Anon., 'Noise in Hospital', *British Medical Journal*, 4:5893 (1973), 625; NHS at 70, Alexa Warnes interview, NHSat70_AlexaWarnes_28052020; NHS at 70, Joan Stevenson interview, NHSat70_JoanStevenson_09012019.

[108] British Library Sound Archive, Interview with Stephanie Pennell by John Newton, 2009, Unheard Voices: interviews with deafened people project (Hearing Link), reference C1345/ 42, track 1, p. 4 of interview transcript.

[109] It is important to remember that sound was perceived in many ways other than through the ears, including as vibration. For some people with hearing impairment, sound might be perceived *only* or *primarily* through the body. On vibration and affect, see Michael Gallagher, 'Sound as Affect: Difference, Power and Spatiality', *Emotion, Space and Society*, 20 (2016), 42–8.

devices. The ICU emerged largely out of the needs of the Second World War and a subsequent polio epidemic, therefore aligned with the NHS itself as a new space and specialism.[110] ICUs had distinct soundscapes. As one *BMJ* article noted in 1979, the nature of illness and extent of sedation in ICU patients meant that 'staff had to speak to the patients loudly, often, and with apparent severity'.[111] The ICU also demanded particularly close monitoring of the vital signs of patients, which first took the form of analogue electrocardiographic monitors (ECGs), then digital monitors that could trigger an alarm rather than requiring monitoring. In the 1960s, the computer technology underpinning ECGs was developed, allowing a range of arrhythmia – beyond catastrophic – to trigger alarms. In 1971, the invention of a microprocessor created what Barro *et al.* describe as a 'quantum leap' towards computers 'suitable for use in bedside equipment'.[112] The number and loudness of alarms proliferated, contributing to a complex psychiatric condition or form of delirium known as 'ICU syndrome'.[113]

Companies that made such technologies tweaked their alarm systems over time in order to tackle the problem of alarm fatigue among staff. The early ECG devices of the 1960s were fairly basic, but newer models incorporate patient data and have a 'triage' system of alarms that produced different pitches and with different sound patterns so that medical staff can distinguish between urgent and non-urgent alerts. In 2002, for example, the Phillips IntelliVue Patient Monitoring system had a 'Red' alarm with a 'high pitched sound, repeated once per second ... clinically significant, potentially life threatening', a 'Yellow ... lower pitched sound, repeated every two seconds ... some clinically significant / life threatening alarms', a 'Yellow-short ... some audible indicator as for yellow alarms, but shorter duration ... related to ECG rhythm' and an 'inoperative' tone.[114] Many of these alarms would be triggered concurrently in shared wards.

New alarms not only changed the soundscape of the hospital, they also demanded different ways of listening. Distinguishing between alarms became increasingly important as, to quote an interview with a Glasgow nurse for the 'NHS at 70' project, alarms have proliferated over time but 'we haven't got the

---

[110] Senen Barro, Jesus Presedo, Paulo Félix, Daniel Castro and Jose Antonio Vila, 'New Trends in Patient Monitoring', *Disease Management and Health Outcomes*, 10:5 (2002), 291–306.

[111] David S. Shovelton, 'Reflections on an Intensive Therapy Unit', *British Medical Journal*, 1:6165 (1979), 737.

[112] Barro *et al.*, 'New Trends', 293.

[113] Anetth Granberg, Ingegerd Bergbom Engberg and Dag Lundberg, 'Intensive Care Syndrome: A Literature Review', *Intensive and Critical Care Nursing*, 12:3 (1996), 173–82; Avinash Konkani and Barbara Oakley, 'Noise in Hospital Intensive Care Units – A Critical Review of a Critical Topic', *Journal of Critical Care*, 27:5 (2012), 522e1–e9.

[114] Rob B. Way, Sally A. Beer and Sarah J. Wilson, 'What's That Noise? Bedside Monitoring in the Emergency Department', *International Emergency Nursing*, 22:4 (2014), 198.

staff to go and see what the alarm's about'.[115] In the ICU, she notes, specific sounds trigger a reaction: 'when you hear that bing bong everybody's up to see what's happened'.[116] Hearing the nuances of technological sounds, as well as patients' voices, required staff to develop new listening practices that might vary across spaces and specialisms. Listening practices also varied between staff, patients and visitors. Changes to patterns or tones of ICU alarms were an important part of maintaining staff attention, but could cause great anxiety to patients alert enough to engage with them. As one patient memoir observed, of his time in a London ICU in the 1990s, 'I got used to their patterns and didn't like it if they went off irregularly.'[117] The rhythmic nature of sounds thus helped to produce the emotional qualities of space. The 'pattern' of high-technology spaces could actually be reassuring, but some patients learned to tune into these sounds and be disturbed by disruptions to them. As with Gleeson's discussion of the air-conditioning unit, given enough time in a space, patients developed new and active relationships to their soundscapes.

Sound-producing technologies were increasingly important for diagnosis, as well as for monitoring patients' health. Many of these sounds were a by-product of the diagnostic process, rather than a part of it. The magnetic resonance imaging (MRI) machine, for example, was first used in the late 1970s and makes a distinctive, loud banging sound caused by pulses of electricity moving through metal coils. Patients lie down in the MRI machine for between fifteen and ninety minutes, creating a particular spatial-sensory experience of the hospital in which the MRI machine becomes their environment and the room outside is irrelevant; in such diagnostic processes, the soundscape is produced by a relationship between a single body and a single machine. In my own study of the senses in recent cancer memoirs, I argued that people hear and give meaning to the rhythmic banging of the MRI machine in relation to their health, illness or emotions at a given time.[118] It is not unreasonable to assume that the same applies to historical subjects.

Other technologies used sound as part of the diagnostic process. Some of these objects had long histories, such as the stethoscope, but were still important for many clinical staff who used them regularly.[119] They gave medics access to a privileged hospital soundscape: the interior of the body. The stethoscope was also supplemented by traditional forms of 'percussion', or tapping on body

---

[115] NHS at 70, Beverley Tiplady interview, NHSat70_BeverleyTiplady_14052019.

[116] NHS at 70, Tiplady

[117] Ben Watt, *Patient: The True Story of a Rare Illness* (Penguin, 1996), p. 52.

[118] Victoria Bates, 'Sensing Space and Making Place: The Hospital and Therapeutic Landscapes in Two Cancer Narratives', *Medical Humanities*, 45:1 (2019), 10–20.

[119] Rice, *Hearing the Hospital*, discusses the stethoscope at length, including how it changes the experience of listening.

parts, which maintained importance in diagnosis and education as a dual act of touch-listening and spatial exploration.[120] In the late twentieth century, new diagnostic machines also used sound waves to create bodily images or to pick up sounds inaudible to the human ear. Such technological advances created a new form of hospital hearing in which machines did the 'listening' and reported sound back to medical technicians and consultants in visual form. Ultrasound, for example, was used for obstetric purposes from the 1950s and became more common in hospitals in the 1960s. In her work on entanglements of matter and meaning, Karen Barad notes that 'when sound waves reflected from different body parts impinge on the transducer, they are converted into electric signals that are visually displayed' but that 'producing a "good" ultrasound image is not as simple as snapping a picture; nor is reading one'.[121] Here, the materiality of sound waves and the ultrasound apparatus are active agents in the production of meaning, in dialogue with the person using the apparatus. The ultrasound provides an example of the importance of sound waves in NHS hospital care, and of the role of new technologies in mediating and 'reading' the soundscapes of bodily interiors.

New technologies reshaped every part of the NHS soundscape, even beyond the 'high-technology' spaces discussed so far. Communication devices, for example, shifted away from the traditional tones of the bedside bell. Early systems in the NHS often constituted a simple buzzer system, which were refined by the 1970s with a system of lights to help staff to identify the exact bed from which a 'call' came.[122] As one interviewee for the 'NHS at 70' project noted, such buzzers could end up being used by lonely patients 'just to see a face', particularly those in single rooms.[123] As with many of the trends noted in this section, private rooms solved some problems while creating others. Designing sound levels 'too low', one acoustic consultant noted, might leave patients 'cut off from the outside world'.[124] The flow of sound was important to a sense of spatial and human connection: when sound was isolated, so were people. For many patients, silence was no more desirable than noise. New spaces and acoustic materials could thus contribute to issues of sensory understimulation, boredom and loneliness, which could be as much of a problem as sensory overload. Some hospitals tried to provide aural connection through

---

[120]   Anna Harris, 'Listening-Touch, Affect and the Crafting of Medical Bodies through Percussion', *Body & Society*, 22:1 (2016), 31–61.

[121]   Karen Barad, *Meeting the Universe Halfway: Quantum Physics and the Entanglement of Matter and Meaning* (Duke University Press, 2007), p. 202.

[122]   Anon, 'Casscom at the Charing Cross Hospital, Fulham', *Hospital Development*, 2:1 (1974), 12.

[123]   NHS at 70, Tiplady.

[124]   Alan Saunders, 'The Sound of Silence', *Hospital Development*, 24:10 (1993), 41.

telephones for patients in single rooms, or at the bedside in wards, but this was an uneven practice and much more common in the private sector. Despite the growing popularity of mobile phones in the 1990s, most NHS Trusts banned them until 2009, due to fears that they would interfere with medical equipment.

Other changes to communications included pager technology, which was patented in 1949, developed in the 1950s and incorporated into hospitals over subsequent decades. Hospital pagers reached the peak of their popularity in the 1980s. An article in a hospital design journal, on the subject of '25 Years of Paging', later noted that selective radio paging was invented by hospitals to overcome noise, as part of a collaboration between St Thomas' Hospital in London and the firm Multitone in 1955. The article also observed that these systems had unanticipated implications for the soundscapes of hospitals: early 'systems were apt to interfere with dictating machines, public address and hearing aids'.[125] In 2019, there were still over 130,000 pagers in use in the NHS, albeit alongside a pledge to phase them out by 2021.[126] The common trend for most hospital communication devices is that they became both more complex and more portable over time. These devices changed the spatiality of hospital sound by moving around with medical staff and patients, in theory reducing disturbances to patients caused by phones and tannoy systems. Individuals in hospitals could be contacted in quiet, more discrete ways, but mobile devices did not simply eliminate sound. Instead, they brought the sounds of communication into personal space. Such devices also created new forms of embodied emotion. As Adèle Bourbonne notes, 'sound ... can trigger a physical and emotional response. Sound startles us, alerts us, orients us'.[127] This emotional aspect of hospital soundscapes is particularly significant for alarms and pagers, with their distinct tones that often marked the arrival of urgent or troubling news.

1.6 Entertainment

Over time, the soundscape of the modern hospital was increasingly filled with the same kinds of entertainment found in the modern city: speakers, radios and televisions. Initiatives to introduce music have a long history in hospitals. Some Victorian asylums and hospitals had a bandstand for live performances, and in the twentieth century, technologies allowed for much wider dissemination of music throughout hospital spaces. In 1924, *The Lancet* reported on the wartime

---

[125] Anon., 'Communications Systems Feature', *Hospital Design*, 9:4 (1981), 19–20.

[126] BBC, 'NHS Told to Ditch "Outdated" Pagers', 23 February 2019, www.bbc.co.uk/news/technology-47332415 (accessed: 8 January 2021).

[127] Adèle Bourbonne, 'Tactile Sound' in Ellen Lupton and Andrea Lipps, eds, *The Senses: Design beyond Vision* (Princeton Architectural Press, 2018).

'substitution of nice noise for horrible noise' in hospitals through gramophones and concerts.[128] In 1948, the Council for Music in Hospitals was formed, at first as an initiative to provide music to wounded servicemen but later expanding its remit. By the 1960s, hospitals were inspired by the commercial sphere and explored the potential of piped music (or 'muzak') in communal areas such as waiting rooms.[129]

Sound design was broadly distinct from noise abatement, but initiatives such as muzak blur the lines. Muzak is often thought of as 'mood music', contributing to a commercial atmosphere and seeking to lift people's moods.[130] Rowland Atkinson notes that the 'blandness of muzak' was also often used in workplaces 'to "smooth" music of its shifts in volume and temp to avoid direct attention'.[131] It is no coincidence that music perceived as calming, such as classical music, was a common choice. As the more extensive discussion of waiting room music in Section 2 shows, though, even within such carefully curated sound design, one person's music could be another person's 'noise'. 'Piped music' can also impede the communication of people with hearing aids, to the extent that the National Institute for the Deaf have even lobbied against its use in pubs.[132]

Historical sources hint further at ways in which the introduction of muzak changed the atmosphere of hospitals. In a King's Fund survey on a music trial in the early 1960s, for example, a number of questionnaire respondents commented explicitly on the role of music in the making of the waiting room atmosphere. These comments can be grouped into two main categories. The first category praised the music for distracting from an unpleasant atmosphere; for example, patients commented that, 'I enjoy the music, and [it] removes the severe atmosphere' and it '[b]rightens an otherwise tense atmosphere, especially if one is rather nervous or apprehensive.'[133] These kinds of comments gave an insight into what patients thought of the 'normal' atmosphere of the outpatients' waiting room: 'severe' and 'tense'. A second group of comments focused on what music added, rather than what it removed: 'music makes a hospital more like home'; 'I think it gives a friendly atmosphere to the hospital'; 'I think it is

[128] Anon., 'Nice Noise', *The Lancet*, 204:5283 (1924), 1139.
[129] Muzak is used here without capitalisation to refer to all background music, not just the specific brand.
[130] James Ingham, Martin Purvis and D. B. Clarke, 'Hearing Places, Making Spaces: Sonorous Geographies, Ephemeral Rhythms, and the Blackburn Warehouse Parties', *Environment and Planning D: Society and Space*, 17:3 (1999), 287.
[131] Rowland Atkinson, 'Ecology of Sound: The Sonic Order of Urban Space', *Urban Studies*, 44:10 (2007), 1911.
[132] Atkinson, 'Ecology of Sound', p. 1908. In 2017 the National Autistic Society also launched a campaign for an 'Autism Hour' in shops, which includes turning off background music.
[133] LMA, London, 'Background Music in Hospitals', A/KE/I/01/01/001, A/KE/I/01/01/010.

a marvelous [sic] idea, it makes a very homely atmosphere not like hospitals years ago'; and '[e]xtremely pleasant making for a more homely atmosphere.'[134]

The focus on 'homely atmospheres' opens up new ways of thinking about sound. The sonic qualities of 'homeliness' differed across time and place, for example, with the rise of suburban living and changes to technologies found in the home.[135] The bustling environment of a crowded Victorian home differed from that of orderly and private ideals of post-war domesticity, for example. These differences might have (re)shaped what kind of hospital space *felt* homely and the role that sound played in this atmospheric production.[136] The definition of a 'home' was of course also highly individual; at least one post-war researcher showed that patients with noisy homes made fewer noise complaints, and the music played in homes would have varied significantly at any given time.[137] In the quoted comments, it seems likely that simply the presence of music – rather than its specific acoustic qualities – represented 'homeliness' at a time when music was rarely heard in public spaces. The meaning of background music changed over time, as it was used more widely in commercial spaces.[138] It therefore cannot be assumed that background music evoked the same feelings of 'homeliness' in 1990s waiting rooms as in the 1960s. As muzak became commonplace, waiting room music may have started to evoke an atmosphere of consumption.

Hospital radio stations also grew in popularity in the UK in the wake of the Second World War and reached a peak with over 350 such stations in the 1980s, although this number has since waned due to funding, hospital mergers and the rise of personal music devices.[139] Scholars of radio have emphasised that it is more than 'background sound'. Despite its 'one to many' formulation, Kimberley Peters argues, radio is an 'intimate' listening experience because of its 'inclusion in daily routines and habits'.[140] Listening routines from home could be brought into the hospital space, helping to remove some of the clinical feel of a space.

---

[134] LMA, London, 'Background Music', A/KE/I/01/01/001, A/KE/I/01/01/004, A/KE/I/01/01/014, A/KE/I/01/01/017.

[135] On noise, homes and suburbs, see Brandon LaBelle, *Acoustic Territories: Sound Culture and Everyday Life* (Bloomsbury, 2010), pp. 32–60.

[136] Claire Langhamer, 'The Meanings of Home in Postwar Britain', *Journal of Contemporary History*, 40:2 (2005), 341–62.

[137] Cecily Statham, 'Noise and the Patient in Hospital: A Personal Investigation', *British Medical Journal* (5 December 1959), 1247–8. This article was also an appendix in The National Archives, London, 'Noise in Hospitals', MH 146/44.

[138] On the 'consumer' aspect of using music as part of noise abatement, see Charles Spence and Steve Keller 'Medicine's Melodies: On the Costs & Benefits of Music, Soundscapes, & Noise in Healthcare Settings', *Music and Medicine*, 11:4 (2019), 211–25.

[139] BBC, 'Whatever Happened to Hospital Radio?', 3 September 2012, www.bbc.co.uk/news/magazine-19270013 (accessed: 8 January 2021).

[140] Kimberley Peters, *Sound, Space and Society: Rebel Radio* (Springer, 2018), p. 52.

Depending on the location of radios in hospitals, their communal nature could also be important. In shared spaces such as day rooms, hospital radio was sometimes played through loudspeakers and provided activities such as bingo or quizzes as well as music.

Hospital televisions were also often viewed communally and located in special rooms. Louise Hide notes that these rooms helped to 'contain noise' from the television but also 'contained' patients and could isolate them away from the ward.[141] Televisions could, like radio, bring routines from home into healthcare spaces; by the 1950s a third of households had a television, a figure that rose to over 90 per cent by the 1970s.[142] Televisions could contribute to atmospheres of care and homeliness for people in long-term care or long-stay wards, but they did not *automatically* do so. As one letter to the *BMJ* observed in 1974, 'television sets and transistor radios in hospital wards ... are a must for convalescing patients, [but] to the still ill patient they are a menace'.[143] Such technologies needed to be carefully situated, to be considerate of the needs of different patient groups, and integrated into what Hide describes as a 'triadic relationship between patient, television, and staff'.[144]

The spatial-acoustic environment was changed by the ability to use bedside headphones in wards, for televisions and radios, which had been available in some hospitals since the 1920s and remained widespread under the NHS. In 1960, the Committee on the Problem of Noise in Hospitals quoted contemporary literature on noise reduction that advised the more widespread use of headphones, as well as noting the existence of other technologies that brought listening into personal space such as 'under-pillow attachments for radio or television sound'.[145] Later, more widely available personal music devices enabled patients to be in an individualised and/or mobile soundscape. Shuhei Hosokawa notes, writing on the 'Walkman Effect', that mobile and personal listening technologies created a form of '"de-territorialised listening" ... every sort of familiar sound-scape is transformed by that singular acoustic experience'.[146] Heike Weber also argues that 'mobile music listening' was never 'passively' consumed, but that such technologies still transformed people's spatial experiences of listening and

[141] Louise Hide, 'The Uses and Misuses of Television in Long-Stay Psychiatric and "Mental Handicap" Wards, 1950s–1980s', in Monika Ankele and Benoît Majerus, eds, *Material Cultures of Psychiatry* (transcript-Verlag, 2020), p. 197.

[142] BBC, 'Number of UK Homes with TVs Falls for First Time', 9 December 2014, www .bbc.co.uk/news/entertainment-arts-30392654 (accessed: 17 March 2021).

[143] J. M. Anderson, 'Noise in Hospital', *British Medical Journal*, 1:5901 (1974), 248.

[144] Hide, 'The Uses and Misuses of Television', p. 192.

[145] The National Archives, 'Noise in Hospitals'.

[146] Shuhei Hosokawa, 'The Walkman Effect', in Jonathan Sterne, ed., *The Sound Studies Reader* (Routledge, 2012), p. 112.

of watching other people listening.[147] The *mode* of listening in hospitals could be as important as the sound itself, as part of a process of co-production between technology and listener.

Hospital headphones rarely completely eliminated the sounds of the hospital. In theory, headphones gave patients more control over the hospital soundscape by changing the dominant sound to their preferred radio station, music, television show or audiobook. However, the implications of doing so were complex. Listening in this context could ruin somebody's favourite song, or fuse the listening experience with negative memories. As Alan Marsden and Richard Leadbeater emphasise, 'hearing music is not just a sonic experience' but a fully embodied and affective one.[148] One cancer patient, treated in Scotland in the early 2000s, recently reported in an interview that:

> The chemo machine ... made this pinging sound. Ping ping pong! ... It drove me crazy ... I did listen to a lot of music then with the headphones on just to blank it out, but even now when I listen to some of the songs that I listened to then, I can hear the pinging going on in the background. It triggers a memory.[149]

Listening to songs in hospital changed their meaning for this patient. Specific music became fused – in this memory – with the unpleasant background sounds of hospital treatment, to the extent that this interviewee still actually *hears* the sounds of the hospital when listening to the songs today. No hospital sound existed independently of others, nor could they ever completely distract from the context of ill health. Headphones did not 'block out' the hospital; they added yet another new dimension to its complex soundscape.

1.7 Making Sense of Cacophonies

In broad terms, this analysis could be read in support of the Nuffield Trust's complaint that hospitals have recently been getting 'steadily noisier'. Their 1955 publication *Studies in the Function and Design of Hospitals* observed that '[t]here is more nursing and medical activity because more patients are in an acute condition, and the sources of noise have increased ... Compact planning has brought these sources of noise nearer to the patient, and the lighter, panel walls and partitions of modern framed structures are less resistant to sound.'[150]

---

[147] Heike Weber, 'Stereo City: Mobile Listening in the 1980s', in Matthew Gandy and B. J. Nilsen, eds, *The Acoustic City* (Jovis, 2014), p. 158.

[148] Alan Marsden and Richard Leadbeater, 'Music: Seeing and Feeling with the Ears', in Ian Heywood, ed., *Sensory Arts and Design* (Bloomsbury, 2017), p. 157.

[149] NHS at 70, Peter McDade interview, NHSat70_PeterMcDade_14062019.

[150] Nuffield Provincial Hospitals Trust, *Studies in the Functions and Design of Hospitals*, p. 115.

This section has identified many of the same phenomena, further showing that many of these trends continued in the years after the report. However, it is limiting to only think of the hospital becoming more or less 'noisy'. The NHS hospital's cacophony was *qualitatively* distinct from that of earlier decades or even centuries. The sounds described by the Nuffield Trust bear little resemblance, for example, to the noises identified by Jonathan Reinarz in the eighteenth-century hospital: from prayers to 'the incessant peal of bells'.[151] They also differed from the 'noise' of the 1930s hospital: '[P]iano, loud-speaker -gramophone, door-bell, ambulance noises, another gramophone, howls from infants' wards, groans from men's wards, chapel organ on Sundays, nurses' rising bell, noises from kitchen and bathroom two yards away, comings and goings of all and sundry.'[152] To describe the post-war hospital just as 'noisy' is to miss the ways that hospital soundscapes – and the sounds identified as noise – changed in nature.

A picture can be painted of the gradual shift to NHS hospital soundscapes over time, or a change to what David Theodore describes as the 'aural profile' of specific spaces.[153] There was some continuity and many changes to the sounds produced in hospitals, the ways in which they moved or intermingled, and the times of day in which the sounds waxed and waned. The hospital had long been a space of cacophony, albeit interspersed with sub-spaces and periods of quiet, but in the NHS hospital specific elements of that cacophony changed: some sounds disappeared from communal spaces with less reverberant buildings, closed windows, new ward layouts, quieter materials such as plastic, the rise of personal listening devices and the shift to out-of-town hospitals; other sounds emerged with new communicative or bedside monitoring devices, new movement patterns around large hospitals, new diagnostic technologies, the rise in traffic outside hospitals and new elements of building infrastructure such as air conditioning. The nature and cultural contexts of those *perceiving* sound also changed.

Despite these broad trends, this discussion has also shown that the NHS hospital portfolio was extremely diverse, and that each hospital had a wide range of spaces within which the soundscape might fluctuate dramatically over the course of a day. There were also many different 'listeners' in any given time and place, each of whom would have heard in specific ways and not just along simple lines, such as staff/patient/visitor. Staff roles shaped their movement around the hospital and listening experiences in a given space, from nurses attuned to the sounds of alarms, to doctors listening out for their pagers, and

---

[151] Reinarz, 'Learning to Use Their Senses', p. 510.
[152] Anon., 'The Woes of a Hospital Resident', *The Lancet*, 224:5792 (1934), p. 513.
[153] Theodore, 'Sound Medicine', p. 987.

estates staff alert to the sounds of the building. Patients and visitors heard the hospital in individual ways, as well as collective ones, which could be shaped by factors ranging from illness to emotional states and personal memories.

These findings pose challenges for historians because they emphasise the complexity of hospital soundscapes and the diversity of listening experience. As Charles Hirschkind notes, 'the historical time of the senses' is specific and does not necessarily align with the discipline's requirements: 'the senses are not a stable foundation ... both perceived objects and perceiving subjects are sensorially plural, enfolding a set of possibilities'.[154] How can historians allow for change over time *and* for the diversity of soundscapes – including the many ways in which they are experienced and given meaning – in any given location? One option is to focus on the social and communal elements of both making and hearing sound. There were changes over time to hospital sound-scapes, the ways in which they were managed, the different actors who (re)shaped them, and the social relations and power dynamics underpinning these processes. The next section addresses some of these issues, as it examines how and why sound was redefined as 'noise'. Such an approach allows histor-ians to find some structure in unstable soundscapes by focusing on the influence of social categories, including gender, race, age and class.

The concept of 'atmosphere' might also enable historians to find order in a complicated picture. 'Atmosphere' *includes* human relations but is not a purely social concept. This analysis has referred to 'atmospheres' already on a few occasions, but has not yet defined the term, partly because it is a fairly ambiguous concept that is used in a wide range of ways. Shanti Sumartojo and Sarah Pink describe an atmosphere as 'a quality of specific configurations of sensation, temporality, movement, memory, our material and immaterial sur-rounds and other people'; together, these factors produce the feeling and meaning of a place or event.[155] To further cite Deborah Lupton on 'affective atmospheres', they are 'often felt or sensed by humans entering a place rather than directly observed or represented in words or images'.[156] Atmospheres shift, with the changing 'configurations' or constellations in a space. There is also some collective quality to atmospheres, which have always been shaped in part by culture, politics and society.[157] As Andreas Rauh argues, a given space

[154] Charles Hirschkind, 'Cassette Sermons, Aural Modernities and the Islamic Revival in Cairo' in Jonathan Sterne, ed., *The Sound Studies Reader* (Routledge, 2012), p. 61.

[155] Sumartojo and Pink, *Atmospheres*, p. 6.

[156] Deborah Lupton, 'How Does Health Feel? Towards Research on the Affective Atmospheres of Digital Health', *Digital Health*, 3 (2017), 10.

[157] Alice Salimbeni, 'A Workshop to Reflect on a Possible Mediation between Affective and Political Atmospheres' in Damien Masson, ed., *Proceedings of the Fourth International Congress on Ambiances* (Réseau International Ambiance, 2020), hal–03136469.121.

or place – at a given point in time – might have 'an' atmosphere as singular (not 'felt *in* a room, but intersubjectively felt *as* a room') or plural atmospheres ('if two people attend the same party, it is possible that they do not speak about the very same atmosphere').[158]

In relation to healthcare, the concept of 'atmosphere' has recently been productive for sociologists and ethnographers. A number of scholars have shown how atmospheres of 'care' are produced through design, social practices and other 'configurations' in space and time.[159] 'Care' is of course a human concept, and this kind of angle differs subtly from the work of scholars interested in atmosphere as something 'in-between' and unnamed.[160] However, scholars of health, space and the senses must pose questions about human feeling and perception at least to some extent. Questions such as those posed about 'care' allow for an understanding of which 'configurations' produce certain atmospheric qualities for patients and staff. While 'care' itself is a human concept, the 'configurations' that produce it include 'material and immaterial surrounds' alike. For historians, it is significant that there is change over time in both the 'configurations' found in hospitals and in the concept of 'care'. There is potentially great value in a more historically oriented approach to such atmospheres, as the shifting social and cultural meanings of 'care' are one part of the ever-changing 'configurations' found in hospital spaces. This approach builds on some of the social approaches already outlined, but recognises social relations as *one* element in shifting 'configurations' of healthcare spaces, which also includes material components.

Social historians might be particularly inclined to ask how hospital atmospheres, and their sensory qualities, were understood and given meaning. They might also lean towards questions about how atmospheric *ideals* were brought into being or 'staged' at different points in time, irrespective of the success of these efforts.[161] These are somewhat natural questions for scholars interested in change over time, and are certainly important questions. The next section follows these lines of enquiry, considering ideas about 'good' and 'bad' soundscapes. It shows that acoustic *design* and attempts to curate hospital soundscapes – successful or not – can be highly revealing about principles of care and

---

[158] Andreas Rauh, *Concerning Astonishing Atmospheres: Aisthesis, Aura and Atmospheric Portfolio* (Mimesis International, 2018), p. 42.

[159] Daryl Martin, Sarah Nettleton and Christina Buse, 'Affecting Care: Maggie's Centres and the Orchestration of Architectural Atmospheres', *Social Science & Medicine*, 240 (2019): 112563; Shanti Sumartojo, Sarah Pink, Melisa Duque and Laurene Vaughan, 'Atmospheres of Care in a Psychiatric Inpatient Unit', *Design for Health*, 4:1 (2020), 24–42.

[160] Mikkel Bille, Peter Bjerregaard and Tim Flohr Sørensen, 'Staging Atmospheres: Materiality, Culture, and the Texture of the In-between', *Emotion, Space and Society*, 15 (2015), 31–8.

[161] Bille, Bjerregaard and Flohr Sørensen, 'Staging Atmospheres'.

power relations in hospitals. The concept of 'atmospheres' also offers a more complex and equally significant line of enquiry for historians. There is great value in recognising that hospital 'atmospheres' could be produced, embodied and historically contingent *without* necessarily being cognised.

There is much work that can be done on sound as part of 'configurations of sensation'. Tim Ingold argues that 'sound ... is neither physical nor psychic but atmospheric', and that thinking atmospherically allows us to think about sound not just as something that travels 'from source to recipient' but as something that 'swirls ... between the two as a river between its banks'.[162] This allows for a conception of sound that moves beyond the hearing of single *objects* ('here a dog barking, there a car-engine running') to incorporate sounds that are cacophonies, 'scrambled', 'diffuse'.[163] This approach might help to resolve some of the difficulties faced in this section, in which it has been difficult to communicate the *qualities* of sound without relying on the reader's familiarity with the objects or sources of sound. It emphasises that sound – and in the case of this section, dynamic layers of different sounds – is a swirling atmospheric quality, rather than something found in a specific object. The combined atmospheric quality of these 'swirling' sounds is perhaps more important than their individual pitch, reverberation, volume or other acoustic qualities.

Kimberley Peters similarly makes a case for the role of sound in atmospheres. She notes that 'sound comes together with subjects, objects, events, memories, moments, places, spaces, and times to create moments of crescendo and silence that generate spatial atmospheres that are felt and lived'.[164] Hospital cacophonies, with their 'moments of crescendo and silence', were part of the co-production of the hospital atmosphere(s). This section has pointed to examples of how affective qualities of sound related to the 'subjects, objects, events, memories' of patients. As Sumartojo and Pink argue, atmospheres do not '*make* people feel particular things ... [I]t is the way that people feel about things that make atmospheres perceptible.'[165] Soundscapes have always shaped how hospitals feel to those who inhabit them and how people *feel about sound* has made 'atmospheres perceptible'. To think 'atmospherically' is thus not to abandon interest in human experience but to understand this experience as a relational process.

The history of hospital cacophonies offers a starting point from which to explore the different atmospheric possibilities of NHS hospitals. Based on the trends outlined in this section, for example, it might be productive to ask: How

---

[162] Tim Ingold, *The Life of Lines* (Routledge, 2015), pp. 106–8.
[163] Ingold, *The Life of Lines*, pp. 106–8.   [164] Peters, *Sound*, p. 61.
[165] Sumartojo and Pink, *Atmospheres*, p. 5.

did 'moments of crescendo and silence' shape the atmosphere(s) of high-technology spaces? How did sound contribute to the atmosphere of communal spaces, including in relation to other design features such as the visual privacy created by curtains around hospital beds? How did the sounds of routines, such as cleaning and serving food, shape the temporality of hospital atmospheres? When atmospheres *were* named or given meaning, what 'configurations of sensation' constituted 'modernity', 'homeliness' or 'care'? How did all of these change over time, and why? There will always be a few different answers to these questions, because each changing soundscape produced a cluster of possible atmospheres. However, the possibilities were not infinite. The concept of 'atmosphere' might enable historians to make some order out of what appears otherwise to be the unstable, shifting sands of relational cacophonies of sound in NHS hospitals.

2 Measurement

Many sounds made up the cacophony of the hospital, but a few rose above the din. They did so for a range of reasons, including loud volume, high pitch, long reverberation, the 'annoyance' factor and what Karin Bijsterveld describes as the 'sonic chaos' of varying rhythm.[166] Some of these sounds came to be measured, identified and labelled as 'noise', often as part of NHS noise abatement strategies that fundamentally shaped hospital buildings and care. It is to this question of 'noise' that this analysis will now turn: which of the sounds outlined in Section 1 were defined as 'noise' and why? How was noise measured, and how did this measurement shape the ways in which it was conceptualised and tackled?

This section focuses on how 'noise' was measured, defined and tackled by two main groups who dominated discussions on hospital noise abatement: those who dealt with the physical structure of hospitals, such as architects and engineers; and those who focused on patient experience, including some medical researchers and the King's Fund charity.[167] It shows that those who conceptualised noise as a measurable phenomenon tended to seek material solutions, while those who conceptualised it in qualitative and social terms tended to focus on behavioural solutions. Taking a social constructivist approach, sounds were made into 'noise' through different measurement processes, actually producing two quite distinct problems under the same label.

---

[166] Bijsterveld, *Mechanical Sound*, p. 82.
[167] Medicine was actually rarely the root of noise abatement measures, despite a long history of concerns about the physical and psychological health impacts of noise. As David Theodore argues, 'the solution to sound problems in the hospital was seen to be cultural and material, not medical'. Theodore, 'Sound Medicine', 986.

National 'noise abatement' discussions, enquiries and campaigns did bring quantitative measures such as decibel levels into dialogue with more traditional qualitative accounts of the experience of hospital 'noise'. However, they never formed an interdisciplinary or *shared* definition of noise.

Noise abatement was a careful curation of the hospital cacophony, and the line between sound design and noise abatement was often blurry. Different interest groups tackled specific aspects of the hospital 'noise' problem, with a shared goal of creating restful atmospheres, but never attempted to eliminate sound completely. Peace and quiet were sought after, in line with Juhani Pallasmaa's argument that 'the most essential auditory experience created by architecture is tranquillity'.[168] Silence, however, was to be avoided.[169] This is perhaps surprising considering that, in the late twentieth century, 'silence' was increasingly prized as part of what Matthew Gandy describes as a 'broader critique of modernity'.[170] However, the hospital operated simultaneously as a microcosm of wider society and as a specific environment with its own sensory cultures and connotations. As noted in Section 1, under-stimulation and boredom posed their own problems in the hospital. In healthcare spaces, 'silence' was often conceptualised in specific terms such as 'deathly', 'eerie' and 'sterile'.[171] Those pursuing noise abatement, irrespective of their definition of 'noise', sought solutions in acceptable levels (quantitative) or types (qualitative) of sound rather its complete absence.

2.1 Decibels

Historians of science and technology have long shown that quantifiable phenomena are not necessarily value-free or 'objective'. Most contemporaries also acknowledged the limits of measurement – and the tools available – as a way of understanding noise in the twentieth century. However, many people concerned about hospital noise still latched onto the apparent certainty and clarity provided by numbers as a way to define the problem. As Bijsterveld notes, in relation to noise abatement campaigns, even those conducting research into noise emphasised that 'noise was not the same as annoyance ... however, loudness levels

---

[168] Juhani Pallasmaa, *The Eyes of the Skin: Architecture and the Senses* (John Wiley & Sons, 2012 [1996]), p. 51.

[169] 'Silence' is in inverted commas here because – like 'noise' – it is a social construction and a concept as much as it is an acoustic phenomenon; the complete absence of sound is arguably not possible outside of anechoic chambers. As Karsten Lichau rightly argues, silence is itself a 'complex acoustical practice'; Karsten Lichau, 'Soundproof Silences? Towards a Sound History of Silence', *International Journal for History, Culture and Modernity*, 7 (2019), 840.

[170] Gandy, 'Introduction', p. 12.

[171] LMA, 'Background Music', A/KE/I/01/01/001; Robert Sloane, 'The Healing Arts', *Hospital Development*, 15:5 (1987), 39.

increasingly became the sign of "how bad" the situation was'.[172] Designers, acoustic engineers and architects in particular seemed to be drawn to quantifiable ways of identifying (and resolving) noise problems.

Changing technologies and ways of 'capturing' noise helped to make – and remake – the noise problem over the course of the twentieth century. As Coreen McGuire notes, in relation to the interwar period, 'instruments designed to measure noise actually worked to redefine the meaning of sound'.[173] Emily Thompson similarly argues that, with that the development of electrical measuring instruments in the 1920s, 'not only did it become possible to measure sound, but the tools also stimulated new ways of thinking about it'.[174] In the pursuit of modern soundscapes that represented efficiency, the main architectural interventions to control sound – both outside and within hospitals – at this time involved controlling reverberant sound.[175] There was further research into the spatiality of sound during the Second World War, which brought advances in acoustic science and engineering.[176] There was also an associated investment in ways of controlling sound through acoustic design and engineering. This research gradually fed into architectural acoustics over the course of the late twentieth century, including in the post-war British hospital.

Decibels provided another key numerical definition of 'noise' from the late 1920s onwards.[177] The decibel was a blunt measurement tool but it was quickly adapted to allow for more complexity. The dB(A), for example, allowed for the difference in perception associated with different frequencies. dB(A) Leq measured average sound levels over a period of time, and dB(A) Lmax measured peak sound levels within a given time frame. The 'phon' offered a form of 'subjective' measurement that measured loudness levels as perceived or heard, rather than the level of sound at source or in a given space. New ways of conceptualising these measurements were developed over time, for the specific purposes of managing sound levels in interior spaces. The Noise Rating (NR) Curve, for example, published by the International Organization for

---

[172] Karin Bijsterveld, 'The Diabolical Symphony of the Mechanical Age: Technology and Symbolism of Sound in European and North American Noise Abatement Campaigns, 1900–40', *Social Studies of Science*, 31:1 (2001), 53.

[173] Coreen Anne McGuire, *Measuring Difference, Numbering Normal: Setting the Standards for Disability in the Interwar Period* (Manchester University Press, 2020), p. 107.

[174] Thompson, *The Soundscape of Modernity*, p. 5.

[175] On early twentieth-century hospitals and Walter Sabine, a key figure in the history of reverberation, see Theodore, 'Sound Medicine', 990.

[176] Understanding transmission of sound became a crucial part of locating enemies in wartime; see Bill Addis, 'A Brief History of Design Methods for Building Acoustics', *Proceedings of the Third International Congress on Construction History*, 20–24 May 2009 (Neunplus1, 2009), 1–10.

[177] Robert Hickling, 'Decibels and Octaves, Who Needs Them?', *Journal of Sound and Vibration*, 291: 3–5 (2006), 1202–7.

Standardization in 1973, focused on indoor sounds. Its curve represented the different relationships between frequency (newly measured in Hz instead of cps) and pressure (dB) that would constitute an 'acceptable' sound profile in specific spaces; in short, it showed that a higher pressure would need to be compensated for by a lower frequency to achieve the same 'acceptable' NR value. This curve recognised that 'acceptable sound pressure levels vary by room type and its use' with specific recommendations provided for each type of building or spaces within buildings.[178] The Noise Criterion (NC) Curve worked on a similar principle, although it was developed in the USA and had slightly different values.

The development of noise meters, which gave the ability to quantify sound in a specific location, happened broadly in tandem with the invention of the decibel. Most early examples of the use of noise meters, for measuring urban sound levels, are traced back to noise abatement campaigns in the late 1920s and early 1930s. At this time there were different forms of noise meter, which were all imperfect but transformative technologies, some of which measured the perception of sound while others focused simply on loudness.[179] As Jon Agar writes, these meters were developed in the early twentieth century to overcome the perceived limits of subjective measurements: 'now the physicist or engineer could take outside the laboratory what they hoped to be an unchallengeable instrumental source of expertise'.[180] The materiality of these measuring devices matters. It affected what could be recorded and how. Figure 8 depicts a post-war noise meter held by the Science Museum: the leading portable technology of a precision sound level meter from Copenhagen.

It is clear from this image that even the 'portable' versions of post-war sound level meters were relatively bulky. The similar 'type 2203' version of Brüel & Kjær's precision sound level meter was comparably light at the time, but still weighed 5 kg when attached to an octave filter set, with another 25 kg for the level recorder.[181] It is rarely possible to identify the exact tools used by those measuring hospital noise in the NHS, but it is likely that they used the same mainstream technologies used elsewhere. One of the few reports on hospital noise measurement that mentions specific technology refers to using the 'CEL-160' graphic recorder in 1986, depicted in Figure 9.[182]

---

[178] Anon., 'Noise Ratings', www.acousticcomfort.co.uk/uploads/Noise%20Ratings.pdf (accessed: 16 November 2020).

[179] Bijsterveld, 'Diabolical Symphony'.   [180] Agar, 'Bodies, Machines and Noise', p. 208.

[181] Anon., 'Historical Milestones of a Sound Level Meter', www.bksv.com/en/Knowledge-center /blog/articles/sound/sound-level-meter-history (accessed: 11 January 2021).

[182] Richard L. Soutar and John A. Wilson, 'Does Hospital Noise Disturb Patients?', *British Medical Journal*, 292:6516 (1986), 305.

Figure 8 Precision sound level meter type 2209, 1960–79. © Science Museum/Science & Society Picture Library. Reproduced with permission of the Science & Society Picture Library.

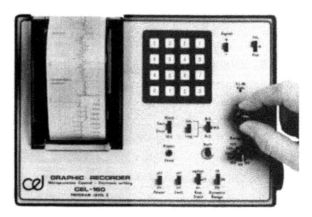

Figure 9 The CEL-160. © Casella. Reproduced with permission of Casella.

The in situ model of the CEL-160 was chosen in this case, despite it being larger than the portable versions available. In order to leave a unit in a room to take measurements, rather than walking a probe around a hospital, a room had to be pre-identified as a potential space of interest. It is significant that many noise meters in hospitals were either positioned in spaces known to be busy or loud (operating theatres, corridors) or where there was a concern about disturbance to patients. This does not necessarily mean that such spaces were noisier but rather that they were identified as spaces – or spaces containing people – of potential interest.

The act of measuring, quantifying and representing decibels changed the way that people thought about the hospital. Noise was not just a problem that was 'out there', finally captured by new technologies; it was also brought into being as a new localised problem *because* of those technologies and the ways in which they represented sound. In July 1980, for example, *HD* reported on the proximity of West Middlesex Hospital to Heathrow Airport's flightpaths: 'the noise level on the roof of the department has been measured at anything up to 95dBA'.[183] Other reports used NR or NC values because of their relevance for defining 'acceptable' sound within a given space. Another *HD* article from 1977 on 'Noise Control' included the 'typical background design levels' for different spaces in the hospitals; the lowest was a single-bed ward at night (NC25) and the highest was 'laboratories, toilets, corridors' (NC40).[184] These figures would have been meaningful to the target readership of hospital designers, engineers and architects.

Few examples of original unprocessed data exist, although the Wellcome Library does hold sound level measurements taken as part of an 'Occupational Health' survey of hospital environmental conditions at Bedford Hospital at some point between the late 1960s and early 1970s.[185] This file takes the form of sound level readings seemingly printed in real time on graph paper, which in consequence is metres in length and shows minute variations in noise levels within even quite short periods of time. Taken as a whole, the graph also shows some more dramatic fluctuations in sound levels over the course of a day. Such data needed to be simplified, arranged and organised into new types of graph for the purposes of analysis, communication and publication. Figure 10 shows a map and a graph from the Nuffield Report's chapter on 'The Control of Sound' (1955), for which noise levels were recorded in a hospital corridor in decibels over a 24-hour period. These graphical representations of decibel levels brought new ways of understanding noise into being. Some graphs in the publication picked out specific moments at which a single loud sound stood out from the average, while others represented frequency and pitch. Taken together, they allowed for a temporal mapping of a soundscape in a given

---

[183] Anon., 'Installations', *Hospital Development*, 8:4 (1980), 15.

[184] J. F. Bridges, 'Noise Control', *Hospital Development*, 5:2 (1977), 29.

[185] Wellcome Library, 'Environmental Assessments of Noise and Temperature in 2 Wards over 24 hours', GC/136/1/6.

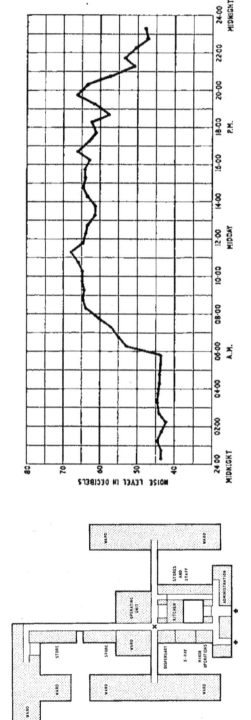

Figure 10 Hospital noise levels, 1955. © The Nuffield Trust. Reproduced with permission of the Nuffield Trust.[186]

[186] Nuffield Provincial Hospitals Trust, *Studies in the Functions and Design of Hospitals*, pp. 115–16.

space and place, albeit within the limits of defining noise in terms of pressure and frequency.

Many publications also offered points of comparison between ideal hospital sound levels and sounds from 'everyday' life, helping to translate abstract numbers into some kind of meaningful qualitative data for non-expert readers. The spaces chosen as comparisons or ideals can be highly revealing of the atmosphere sought in hospitals. Hospitals had a recommended NR value of 30 alongside '[p]rivate dwellings ... theatres, cinemas, conference rooms'. Some specific spaces (at NR35) within hospitals were also identified: 'hospitals operating theatres and wards', compared with the NR values of '[l]ibraries, museums, court rooms ... hotels, executive offices'.[187] These kinds of lists helped to communicate the meaning of NR values. They aligned the 'accept-able' hospital with quiet public spaces alongside a particular idea of civilisation and culture, for example, with the conspicuous mention of 'executive' offices rather than just offices. The 'library' was an apt comparison for the ideal hospital as a restorative place, with its symbolism as an environment of peace, order and calm. At the other end of the scale, undesirable hospital soundscapes were often aligned with the sounds of modernity. The higher ends of the NR scale were compared to 'heavy engineering works'. In Ervin Pütsep's international book *Modern Hospital* (1979), abstract decibel values were made meaningful in relation to very specific reference points from every-day life: a decibel level of 103, with risk of harm, as a 'jet flyover at 305 m', very loud at 85 dB was 'crying babies' and moderate noise at 78 dB was a 'clothes washer', while the noise levels 'accepted by the sick' again were again com-pared to a quiet garden or a public library.[188] These publications translated metrics into meaning, through comparison to value-laden spaces or recognis-able reference points. *Some* of the louder examples given were non-technological, such as babies or orchestras, but overall, undesirable noise levels were more likely to be compared to objects or spaces of technology, industry or modernity, and desirable ones to spaces of nature or culture.

Some high-profile external sources such as the World Health Organization (WHO) recommended maximum decibel levels for hospitals, against which the actual noise levels of a hospital space could be compared. Over the course of the 1970s, the WHO developed recommendations on environmental health criteria for noise, published in 1980. This publication did not specify noise levels for hospitals at first but did give recommendations that hospital planners could use, for example, noting that 'disturbance of sleep becomes increasingly apparent as

[187] Anon., 'Noise Ratings'.
[188] Ervin Pütsep, *Modern Hospital: International Planning Practices* (Lloyd-Luke, 1979), p. 249.

ambient noise levels exceed about 35 dB(A) Leq'.[189] Such measurements spoke
not only to architecture and engineering but also to medicine. Although the
medical profession was never the driving force in hospital noise abatement,
medical journals showed a particular interest in the problem of sleep disturbance, partly in the pursuit of recovery and reducing the amount of time that
patients spent in hospital.[190] When the WHO later published *Guidelines for
Community Noise* in 1999, they included more specific advice for hospitals,
including guideline values for wards of 30 dB(A) Leq and 40 db(A) Lmax at
night.[191]

Target decibel levels were seemingly an ideal. They were based less on
measurements taken from an average hospital space and more on ideas about
how the hospital should sound – or rather how it should *not* sound. Setting this
kind of measurable goal brought noise into being as a problem in the NHS
hospital, as noise meters almost inevitably showed that spaces exceeded the
ideal levels. 'Objective' measurements of hospital noise thus tended to highlight, or even to create, problems in need of a solution. It is also noteworthy that
there was rarely any discussion of who these ideal decibel levels were for. The
person *hearing* noise was often conspicuous by their absence in these discussions. Noise level guidelines implicitly assumed a 'norm' of hearing ability,
which is in itself a problematic concept.[192] There was little attention paid, for
example, to the impact of hearing aids on 'noise' or to people with heightened
sensory perception. Standardising 'noise level' recommendations meant standardising the imagined patient.

When measured in decibels, noise was the end product of a set of material
processes: sound waves, emitted by people and things; then the amplification,
insulation and/or absorption of these waves by the hospital space; and finally
received by noise meters and human bodies. A sound became noise when it
tipped over recommended decibel levels. Noise was also often a relative concept when measured and quantified in terms such as perceived 'loudness', for
example, there was a general perception that hospitals were getting nois*ier* over
time and that some spaces and times of day were nois*ier* than others. Solving the
problem of measurable noise thus often became a matter of tackling the nois*iest*
phenomena (whether in terms of a space, an object or a particularly problematic

---

[189] World Health Organization, *Noise: Executive Summary-Environmental Health Criteria 12* (World Health Organization, 1980), p. 6.
[190] This focus on sleep meant that medical journals are one of the few sources in which earplug use, rather than noise reduction, was presented as a solution to noise; for example, see J. F. Roberts, 'Noise and Its Effects', *British Medical Journal*, 2:5463 (1965), 702.
[191] Birgitta Berglund, Thomas Lindvall and Dietrich H. Schwela, *Guidelines for Community Noise* (World Health Organization, 1999), p. 44.
[192] On constructions of 'disability' and 'normal' hearing, see McGuire, *Measuring Difference*.

time of day) that was feasible to tackle. There were also implicit value judge-ments, even within measurable definitions of noise, in deciding which spaces merited the investment of time and money for solutions.

2.2 Design

When the noise problem was understood in terms of the material qualities of sound, such as pressure and frequency, it called for material solutions. A chapter entitled 'Control of Noise' in the 1955 Nuffield Trust report demonstrates this close relationship between the conceptualisation of 'noise' as a quantitative problem and proposed design solutions. The Nuffield Trust acknowledged patients' personal preferences, but primarily in the context of an ongoing effort to identify and quantify acceptable 'noise' levels. The report recognised that the 'subjective' aspects of noise perception went beyond physiological factors (such as illness and age) to include influences such as life experience and personal preference. However, the report dedicated much more space to quanti-tative measurements, represented in numerical form, as in the graphs already shown in Figure 10. Their adjustment to the 'subjective' aspect of noise perception was to use the phon as their unit of measurement, which was still ultimately a measure of loudness; there was no effort to redefine noise in qualitative terms. Overall, the Nuffield report measured sound quantitatively, conceptualised the problem of noise in terms of loudness and ultimately sought solutions in the reduction of sound levels.

As the Nuffield Trust's publication was on the subject of hospital buildings, it is no real surprise that its proposed solutions to reduce noise were drawn from architecture and acoustic engineering. There was very little new hospital build-ing taking place at this time, so the recommendations focused on adapting existing 'problem' spaces. The Nuffield Trust chose experimental case study sites, including a ward unit at Larkfield Hospital, Greenock, which 'presented a particularly difficult problem in sound-control … three-quarters of the beds are in open bays divided from each other by partitions, but giving directly on to a central circulation space; the remaining beds are in separate single beds'.[193] The Trust experimented with sound control in this unit, often applying broad recommendations from the government-funded 'Building Research Station' to hospital environments. Sometimes they needed to conduct specific research for this purpose, for example, conducting bacteriological tests of acoustic ceiling panels to ensure their suitability, but generally they used existing acoustic engineering solutions rather than developing new ones. Figure 11 depicts the

---

[193] Nuffield Provincial Hospitals Trust, *Studies in the Functions and Design of Hospitals*, p. 118.

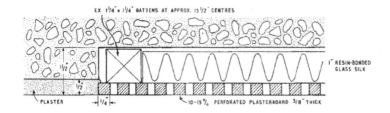

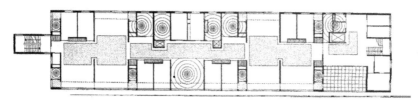

Figure 11 Control of sound at Larkfield Hospital, 1955. © The Nuffield Trust. Reproduced with permission of the Nuffield Trust.[194]

main interventions, showing clearly the emphasis on material solutions to the noise problem (as one of loudness).

This image represents the spatial distribution of sound at different locations within a ward unit. It suggests carefully positioned 'sound-absorbing' ceiling panels made of 'perforated gypsum plaster-board backed with glass silk'. Other recommendations included measuring the qualities of different floor and wall materials in order to reduce sound levels, using a floating floor and introducing cavity walls to provide acoustic insulation between rooms. There were also a few other design recommendations to reduce sounds at source, such as cushioned automatic-closing doors and fibre runners on bed curtains, but these were a relatively minor focus. These experimental wards were metric- rather than experience-driven. The design goal was not necessarily to create a pleasant environment for patients but to reduce disruptive noise for patients and staff alike. The qualitative aspects of the soundscape were much less important for the purposes of a modern and efficient hospital than the amount of sound and reverberation.

Many hospital sites did not have a budget for rebuilding and renovations in the early years of the NHS. As *The Lancet* observed in 1958, 'many sound-proofing schemes are considered impracticable owing to their expense', but there also was an economic incentive to reduce noise if it hastened patient recovery.[195] In consequence, there was also a market for the – apparently simpler and cheaper – solution

---

[194] Nuffield Provincial Hospitals Trust, *Studies in the Functions and Design of Hospitals*, pp. 119–20.
[195] Anon., 'Noise in Hospitals', *The Lancet*, 272:7059 (1958), 1269.

of replacing some hospitals' worst noise culprits, such as squeaky trolleys, creaky doors and clattering crockery. As another *Lancet* article noted three years later, hospitals were very interested in making patients' stays 'shorter and more pleasant' if they could also find cheap and sterile solutions: examples, it suggested, included piped oxygen (rather than cylinders) and plastic doors.[196] In 1963, Hope Hospital in Salford tackled noise in such a budget-friendly way, purchasing rubber lids for bins, anti-rattle pegs on windows and squeak-free trolleys.[197]

New hospital buildings under the Hospital Plan and beyond allowed for solutions such as new ward layouts, quieter wards overlooking courtyards or relocating noisy services. More commonly, in old and new hospitals alike, solutions were sought in the materiality of floors, walls, ceilings and windows. Professional journals often commented on material choices in relation to noise control in hospital renovations. To cite just some examples from *HD* across the decades, in date order: in 1974, there was an article on Ashford Hospital, close to Heathrow airport, that noted noise reduction involving 'double glazed windows, denser roof construction and part air-conditioning'; in 1975, HD reported that Royal Victoria Infirmary in Newcastle, had used an 'acoustic ceiling and carpeting [to] absorb noise' in an open-plan accident and emergency department; and in 1984 it noted that in Milton Keynes DGH, there was widespread use of carpet to 'give comfort, good appearance and reduced noise levels'.[198] Publications of this kind typically conceptualised noise as a material problem to be solved by material means. Noise reduction was represented as a process achieved through double glazing, acoustic flooring and easy-clean carpeting.

Many of these strategies were drawn from wider commercial design. At first, they typically involved strengthening the sound insulation and absorption properties of hospital buildings. In the 1980s, *HD* turned to some new potential solutions drawn from the commercial sector such as 'sound masking' installations. Sound masking was a method of *perceived* noise reduction used more typically in open-plan offices, which raised the base level of sound and thus reduced sharp fluctuations in volume.[199] This alignment with the commercial sector was significant at a time when NHS care and design was drawing increasingly from a consumer model. If the goal of such interventions was an atmosphere of modern, quiet efficiency such as the office, or a commerical atmosphere such as the hotel, it demonstrates a close interplay between NHS principles and acoustic design.

---

[196] Anon., 'Noise in Hospitals', *The Lancet*, 278:2702 (1961), 590.

[197] Anon., 'Cutting Down the Noise in Hospital Wards', *The Guardian*, 9 May 1963, 6.

[198] Anon., 'Ashford Hospital', *Hospital Development*, 2:4 (1974), 37; Anon., 'Minidata: Royal Victoria Infirmary', *Hospital Development*, 3:3 (1975), 44; Anon., 'Milton Keynes DGH', *Hospital Development*, 12:1 (1984), 28.

[199] For example, Tony Smith, 'Sound Masking Advances', *Hospital Development*, 14:2 (1986), 39.

Reports in journals such as *The Hospital* and *HD* often relate to the full
(re)design of a specific hospital building or room, of which acoustic qualities
formed just one part. Occasionally, though, these journals published longer
pieces by acoustic experts on the noise problem and ways to resolve it. Some
of these articles also paid attention to the challenge of tackling sound at source.
One such example was by J. F. Bridges of Sound Research Laboratories Ltd in
1977, who paid extensive attention to recommended noise levels in hospitals
(using NC levels) and the type of material absorption and insulation required to
achieve them.[200] The article addressed the specific concerns of hospital noise
such as reverberation in sterile spaces, the 'impact noise' caused by people and
objects travelling along corridors, and mechanical noise. It offered a range of
highly specific suggestions for tackling the noise problem, ranging from 'perforated metal pan ceilings with bagged glassfibre infill' to 'flexible PVC sheet
which has a foam backing' for flooring in clinical areas where carpet was less
likely to be acceptable.[201] In 1993, *HD* also published an article by an acoustic
consultant that – as with many of the examples already cited – noted that noises
were 'undesirable sounds' and 'need not necessarily be loud', but went on to
focus on measurable 'Noise Rating' curves and sound frequencies.[202] Its
recommendations included identifying the idea level of hospital 'background
noise', which would mask speech without disturbing people, and suggested
engineering and design interventions to achieve this: suspended ceiling tiles, for
example, were 'more effective than carpeting or drapes . . . in terms of noise
absorption per square metre'.[203] The article also suggested that changing
layouts could act as a form of 'masking', allowing hospital noise or traffic to
bleed into certain spaces in a controlled manner to cover the sounds of other
patients in distress.

Many of the articles on noise abatement in *HD* were to some extent advertisements, or at least forms of self-promotion. The reports were often provided
by hospital architects or design companies as examples of successful installations. Even with this in mind, it is significant that material solutions were the
focus of advertisements for successful noise reduction, albeit perhaps not
entirely surprising in a journal aimed at the construction industry. One full
page in *The Hospital* magazine in 1962 showed an advertisement for acoustic
ceilings and partitions: the advert had 'NOISE NOISE NOISE' in large writing,
taking up three-quarters of the page, headed with the text 'The rest is silence
with sound control by Compactom Acoustic Ceilings and Partitions:
Compactom Partitions have been selected for permanent display in the

---

[200] Bridges, 'Noise Control'.   [201] Bridges, 'Noise Control', p. 30.
[202] Saunders, 'The Sound of Silence'.   [203] Saunders, 'The Sound of Silence', p. 41.

Hospital Section at the London Building Centre.'[204] Some adverts pitched sound-reducing redesigns of common hospital objects. In 1961, *The Hospital* ran a half-page advertisement from Lustroid Ltd, which made plastics. It had images of plates, beakers, trays and a 'melamine cup and saucer' for use in wards, with the claim in large text that 'PLASTICS REDUCE NOISE'.[205] Other material solutions were found in adapting the building's infrastructure. In 1977 *HD* ran a full page advertisement for Stanley Automatic Doors, which promoted the 'Stanley Silent Swing ... virtually silent'.[206] This advert again proposed a budget material solution to the problem of noisy doors, offering an automatic door closer (reminiscent of the Nuffield recommendations) as an alternative to the expense of replacing doors. It emphasised silence, energy efficiency and the comparable needs of 'hospitals' and the commercial spaces of 'nursing homes ... hotels ... supermarkets ... offices' and more. This aligns to some extent with the spatial reference points discussed earlier for acceptable NR values in hospitals, which included 'hotels' and 'executive offices'. All of these adverts, like many of the other interventions discussed, focused on loudness, on material solutions and – in line with a consumer model of health-care – on the commercial sphere as design inspiration.

The story of these noise abatement measures further complicates any neat narrative of the modern hospital getting increasingly 'noisy'. Every time a material, acoustic solution was brought into the hospital, it did make the hospital quieter, but loudness was only one part of its soundscape. Returning to the arguments of Section 1, it is also possible to see these inventions as part of the re-making of the hospital soundscape. Some material noise abatement measures made hospitals quieter, but they also introduced new sounds and new spatialities of sound. The introduction of sound absorbing materials, for example, created a cleaner kind of non-reverberant sound. The use of noise masking techniques and technologies might have the opposite effect, absorbing sounds into an unclear auditory fog. Relocating sound-producing rooms away from patients might have made them newly audible to other people in hospitals, particularly members of staff. Noise management that aligned with non-clinical sites, using the materials and methods of offices or hotels, might have produced not only a quieter space but contributed to a new kind of commercial atmosphere.

This section so far, taken all together, argues that quantitative modes of measurement brought noise into being as a material problem of loudness. They came hand-in-hand with material solutions and qualitative definitions of

---

[204] Compactom Ltd, *The Hospital*, October 1962, xlvi.
[205] Lustroid, *The Hospital*, March 1961, xxii.
[206] Stanley, *Hospital Development*, 5:6 (1977), 15.

success, understood as a reduction in decibels of NR values. The structure of this argument might, though, imply a cause-and-effect relationship that is unrealistically linear. Professionals who *already* worked with materials were more likely to reach for measurable understandings of the 'noise problem' in the first place; architects, engineers, designers and those working in hospital estates fell into this category. Their interest in material solutions led to a hunt for material problems, and *vice versa*. Such professionals did not deny that there were qualitative conceptions of noise, but qualitative data was just of less relevance to their own specific professional practice. Material understandings of the noise problem and its solutions also had appeal where they aligned with – and helped to shape – certain visions of the hospital building and the NHS itself, for example, as efficient and modern, and increasingly over time as a place for the 'patient-consumer'.

2.3 Surveys

Noise has never been purely a matter of loudness, nor should it be dismissed as 'meaningless sound'.[207] It is a highly meaningful concept. As environmental historian Peter Coates notes, 'Noise is to sound what stench is to smell (and what weed is to plant) – something dissonant, unwanted, out of place, and invasive.'[208] This comment builds upon the famous work of anthropologist Mary Douglas on 'dirt' as something literally and figuratively 'out of place'.[209] No object carries the inherent quality of being 'dirty', and no sound carries the inherent quality of being 'noisy'; noise is subjective and context-specific. In the post-war period, it was common for complaints about intrusive sound to be framed as 'noise pollution'.[210] Such language reinforced a model of the ideal hospital as a space of sonic purity, albeit not necessarily of silence, which was being slowly destroyed by the infiltration of *unnecessary* sound – another type of sound 'out of place'. This 'noise' was fundamentally social in nature and was brought into being through a different mode of measurement: the questionnaire. Questionnaires revealed changing ideas about appropriate neighbourly behaviour, who had the right to make noise, who had the power to define what was 'necessary', and the rise of patient-centred care. As this analysis will go on to

---

[207] On noise as 'meaningless' sound see Pütsep, *Modern Hospital*, p. 248.
[208] Coates, 'The Strange Stillness of the Past', 643. See also Atkinson, 'Ecology of Sound', 1905.
[209] Mary Douglas, *Purity and Danger: An Analysis of Concepts of Pollution and Taboo* (Routledge and Kegan Paul, 1966).
[210] Philip Radford, 'Noise – Hearing Loss and Psychological', *British Medical Journal*, 282:6257 (1981), 73; Anon., 'Noise in Hospital' (1973).

show, those who conducted qualitative research were much more likely to recommend behavioural interventions as solutions.

Unlike the 'decibel', questionnaires and surveys were not a new measurement device in the twentieth century. Questionnaires as the basis for census data can be seen as far back as the Roman Empire, but they evolved in form, function and purpose over time, and increasingly became tools for social and health analysis rather than simple data gathering. Jon Lawrence argues that it was largely after the First World War that social investigation moved into the professional rather than amateur sphere.[211] The Second World War also led to expansion of government interest in such methods internationally, as a means of understanding the attitudes and experiences of the population.[212] Mass Observation had been launched in the 1930s and ran throughout the war as a way of understanding 'everyday' life. By the post-war period, British people were well versed in interviews, surveys and questionnaires about their experiences and even their feelings. In broad terms, while questionnaires and surveys were not new forms of measurement, there were some shifts over the modern period in how these sources were used: answers moved from being primarily the basis for quantitative analysis to being seen as qualitative data worthy of analysis in their own right.

The history of health research is inextricably interwoven with these trends. Daisy Payling has shown that 'the Second World War and the rise of social medicine encouraged the conception of whole population health as a social problem worthy of social investigation'.[213] As 'health' in general was conceptualised in increasingly social terms, with the rise of social medicine, the qualitative tools of social science and social surveys became ever more important. The use of questionnaires to understand patient *experience* and the social aspects of illness, in particular, was still a relatively novel phenomenon in the mid-twentieth century. Before that time, writings on patient experience were based on observation rather than interview or survey.[214] In 1960s health research, there was a move from these more observational forms of research to a wider range of qualitative research methods that recognised the power

---

[211] The few high-profile studies before this time, such as those of Booth and Rowntree, remained exeptions; Jon Lawrence, 'Class, "Affluence" and the Study of Everyday Life in Britain, c. 1930–64', *Cultural and Social History*, 10:2 (2013), 274.

[212] Charlotte Greenhalgh, 'Social Surveys' in Miriam Dobson and Benjamin Ziemann, eds, *Reading Primary Sources: The Interpretation of Texts from Nineteenth and Twentieth Century History*, 2nd ed. (Routledge, 2020), p. 122.

[213] Daisy Payling, '"The People Who Write to Us Are the People Who Don't Like Us": Class, Gender, and Citizenship in the Survey of Sickness, 1943–1952', *Journal of British Studies*, 59:2 (2020), 316.

[214] Florence Nightingale's comments about noise in *Notes on Nursing*, cited at the start of this Element, are one such example.

dynamics of the process.[215] As Carol Grbich argues, such research also fed into tangible outcomes as a way of 'empowering participants'.[216] This trend aligned more generally with the democratising principles of post-war society, in which civil rights groups called increasingly for an examination of power dynamics and a voice for those often marginalised. By the 1960s, there were a number of patient groups calling for rights within the NHS and meaningful input into the new system. Long-standing organisations such as the King's Fund charity, which led some of the most important noise surveys of the post-war period, were also revitalised by the launch of the NHS. They put extensive resources into understanding ways to improve the system, and to researching the experiences of all of those who used and worked in hospitals.

Not all qualitative research methods should be considered 'equal'. Just as noise meters had limits of form and function, so did questionnaires. Medical researchers often asked only simple questions about noise as a basis for statistical analysis and with a focus on physical or psychological harm, rather than in terms of experience.[217] A few medical professionals did larger-scale qualitative studies, although such research was often localised and driven by personal interest rather than a professional trend. In 1959, for example, an assistant anaesthetist at Royal Northern Hospital in London published an article entitled 'Noise and the Patient in Hospital: A Personal Investigation' which involved verbal interviews of over 100 patients.[218] The Standing Nursing Advisory Committee, around the same time, undertook an unusually extensive medical research project on noise at the request of the Minister of Health. They asked staff and patients to record the 'most bothersome noises', from which they compiled a list of the most prevalent offenders and highlighted those that might be easily eliminated.[219] In general, these medical researchers took more steps than most architects, engineers and designers to use questionnaires in the first place, but the format of such questionnaires limited the degree to which 'noise' could be reconceptualised as a qualitative problem. Even medical discussions about the 'subjective' nature of noise often focused on the influence of measurable phenomena, such as the age of the listener and their distance from the noise source.

Despite the limits of these surveys, even basic questionnaires lent themselves to understanding the patient's perspective. In 1964, for example, a *BMJ* article on the 'Patient's View of Admission to a London Teaching Hospital' reported the following: 'Of 174 patients, 21% complained about noise in our questionary. Those who mentioned the source of the noise were particularly troubled by

[215] Carol Grbich, *Qualitative Research in Health: An Introduction* (Sage, 1998), pp. 8–9.
[216] Grbich, *Qualitative Research in Health*, p. 9.   [217] Mansell, *The Age of Noise in Britain*.
[218] For example, see Statham, 'Noise and the Patient'.   [219] TNA, 'Noise in Hospitals'.

other patients who were very ill or mentally disturbed, and by the telephone ringing at night.'[220] This answer was based on a questionnaire by medics at King's College Hospital, with only one question on noise: 'Did noise worry you much while you were in hospital? No/Yes (specify)'. This type of question was not designed to dig into the subjective nature of noise. The authors went on to compare patients' feedback with decibel levels, in order to assess whether the complaints were justified in relation to measurable phenomena, rather than treating qualitative data as significant in its own right. However, a closer look at the *BMJ* extract shows that the questionnaire lent itself implicitly to definitions of 'noise' that went beyond loudness: the responses hint at the ways that noise was made through temporality ('noise' being perceived more at night) and emotion (being 'troubled' more by ill patients). A 1973 article in the *BMJ* on 'Noise in Hospital' again dedicated most of its discussion of 'noise' to measurable phenomena of 'decibels' and 'Hertz', but based on questionnaires noted that the effect of noise was worse 'if the sounds arouse fear, as groans and cries may'.[221] Questionnaires, by their very nature, elicited responses about the social and emotional dimensions of 'noise'.

Noise was more likely to be reconceptualised as an entirely 'qualitative' problem when the questionnaire was treated as a qualitative measuring tool in its own right, rather than just a basis for calculating statistics or compiling lists of noise sources. The King's Fund, for example, put qualitative data at the core of their practice. In line with the post-war trends in survey methods already outlined, the King's Fund used questionnaires as a social research tool as much as a medical one. They conducted a series of investigations into 'noise', between the 1950s and 1970s, by sending questionnaires to thousands of hospital patients and evaluating the responses. Unlike the medical research cited, these questionnaires gave large areas for free-text answers. The questions stayed relatively consistent over time, asking primarily for details of the noises that 'worried' people. The questionnaires asked for specific examples in categories, such as those 'made by equipment: trolleys, doors, etc'. They also requested details about the noise, such as when it happened and adjectives to describe the sound.[222]

As with any form of measurement, the questions asked would have directly shaped the answers provided. In the King's Fund questionnaire, the questions

[220] P. Hugh-Jones, A. R. Tanser and C. Whitby, 'Patient's View of Admission to a London Teaching Hospital', *British Medical Journal*, 2:5410 (1964), 661.

[221] Anon., 'Noise in Hospital' (1973), p. 625.

[222] King Edward's Hospital Fund for London, *Noise Control in Hospitals: A Report of an Enquiry* (King's Fund, 1958), p. 15; King Edward's Hospital Fund for London, *Noise Control in Hospitals: Report of a Follow-up Enquiry* (King's Fund, 1960), pp. 28–9; M. Dorothy Hinks, *The Most Cruel Absence of Care* (King's Fund, 1974), p. 43.

were often leading; by providing examples of possible sources of 'noise', the design of the questionnaire built in some of the answers that it was anticipating as something of a self-fulfilling prophecy. Looking at the questions posed, it becomes unsurprising that 'trolleys' were one of the most common sources of complaint. The shape of the questionnaire also evolved in response to answers. The additions of 'lifts' and 'crockery' to the list of possible bothersome noises in 1960, for example, reflected and reinforced answers from the previous questionnaire. Questions about the sources of 'noise' might be less significant, though, than the space given to *detail*. The King's Fund questionnaires left large gaps on the page after questions in order to encourage comment and elaboration. They asked for specific details of noises, including prompting respondents to give adjectives to describe sounds. The addition of an 'any other comments' box in 1960 may have reflected the fact that most patients already added some extra comments without invitation.[223] It reinforced this practice and created a space in which patients could bring *any* of their thoughts about hospital 'noise' to the page. The methodological determinism of the questionnaire should not be overstated, as many patients did not use the final box or even complain about noise at all, but these questions encouraged a certain approach to 'noise' among those who did.

These questionnaires quite literally made space for patients' voices, with an assurance of anonymity. They allowed patients to dig a little deeper into why certain noises bothered them, including issues around the temporality of sound and some of the emotional aspects of 'noise' upon which the *BMJ* pieces had briefly touched. The questionnaires allowed patients to go beyond single words and form a narrative of sorts – albeit short and fractured – about their experience of hospitals. This form also allowed the King's Fund to go beyond statistical reports on their answers, to think about responses in terms of language and meaning. The King's Fund reports did provide some tables of statistics that summarised the data, allowing for comparisons over time, but their main focus was on the *words* of respondents. By reporting patients' responses in some detail, the reports placed at their centre the social, cultural and emotional ways in which noise was made and experienced in the NHS hospital. The following discussion draws on these noise surveys, and brings in some responses to questionnaires used in an evaluation of New Guy's House in 1962 in which patients were asked about noise disturbance as part of a bigger survey of new six-bed wards.[224]

---

[223] I have not located original questionnaire responses for the noise surveys, but in other King's Fund questionnaires, patients often made extra comments in margins or overleaf; LMA, 'Completed Questionnaires', A/KE/I/01/24/061.

[224] LMA, 'Completed Questionnaires'.

Responses to the King's Fund questionnaires show that not all (loud) sounds were thought to be 'noises', and that 'noise' was not defined only by loudness. The same sound at the same decibel level could become 'noise' over time, often in line with wider societal conversations. Traffic, for example, was a focal point of political discussions about 'noise pollution', the noise abatement campaigns and patients' complaints about hospital noise in the 1960s. These complaints about traffic tended also to capture newspaper headlines, such as a report in *The Guardian* in 1960 on hospital noise subtitled 'TRAFFIC WORST'.[225] Such complaints actually diminished by the 1970s as patients seemingly got used to the sound of traffic, indicating that noise was defined as much by context as by volume. Patients also rarely bemoaned sound-making medical technologies such as monitoring devices, irrespective of how loud they were, while complaining about quieter – but implicitly unnecessary – sounds made by fellow patients or staff.

When noise was understood in these qualitative terms, of (un)necessary sound, it was also brought into being as a social construct. What – or who – was labelled as 'noisy' reveals ideas of social order in a given time and place, particularly as a relatively narrow group of people were given the power to define 'noise'. The King's Fund questionnaires focused on spaces of waiting or recovery, such as wards, and often did so through a patient-centred lens. The limited attention given to medical staff in these surveys marked a shift in tone away from concerns about efficiency and communication, which had often been staff-oriented concepts even though patient treatment was the ultimate goal. This is not to say that the staff view was completely neglected, as some of the King's Fund surveys on waiting room music included staff. Some took the opportunity to make their own noise complaints, such as bemoaning the difficulty of 'listening to a chest' when music was playing, but there was overall a growing emphasis on the patient's voice in this period.[226] In a 2008 literature review, Ulrich *et al.* noted that there was still a need for more studies of the impact of noise on medical staff, particularly in relation to performance, memory, distraction and error.[227] It is significant that in the same article they could cite multiple studies across previous decades of the impact of 'environmental noise' on patients' sleep.[228] The King's Fund studies were part of this wider trend, in which the power to define 'noise' was placed increasingly in patients' hands.

[225] Anon., 'Noises Off', *The Guardian*, 19 December 1960, 4.

[226] LMA, 'Background Music', A/KE/I/01/01/011.

[227] Roger S. Ulrich, Craig Zimring, Xuemei Zhu *et al.*, 'A Review of the Research Literature on Evidence-Based Healthcare Design', *HERD*, 1:3 (2008), 78.

[228] Ulrich *et al.*, 'Literature Review', p. 82.

The King's Fund questionnaires focused on patient experience, partly as a concern in its own right and partly because rest was thought to be crucial for speedy and successful recuperation. The idea of hospitals as spaces of rest had, though, always been more of an ideal than a reality. Hospitals were places of work, learning and activity. The hospital's role as a site of slow recuperation was also eroded over the course of the late twentieth century. The average period of stay for in-patients (all specialties) dropped from 30.9 days in 1964 to 23.4 by 1973, 8.4 by the end of the century and a mere 4.5 in 2018/19.[229] Many long-stay patients such as those in 'psychiatric' and 'geriatric' units were moved into alternative forms of 'community care'. The King's Fund surveys therefore took place at a specific moment of importance in regard to hospital rest: there was interest in patients' experiences of hospital stays, patients actually *did* stay in hospital for a relatively long period of time, and there was growing pressure on hospital beds. Noise control, with its promotion of a 'restful' atmosphere, trod a careful line at this time: it enhanced 'patient-centred' spaces of care and helped hospital 'efficiency' by promoting rapid recovery. Noise abatement was, though, not simply a process of putting NHS principles into practice. At a key point of transition, the King's Fund research also fed into the values of the NHS and helped to shape what 'patient-centred' care looked (or sounded) like, and how it might be made compatible with the other requirements of hospital work.

Who was 'the' patient, as represented in noise surveys? The King's Fund report acknowledged differences in the needs of patients to some extent, particularly on the basis of age, but in general 'the' patient was an imagined and somewhat homogeneous figure who could never truly embody the diversity of those spending time in the NHS hospital. Patients needed to be able to read and write in English to answer the questions. A number of patients simply observed that they could not respond to a survey about 'noise' because they were 'deaf'. Only one person who described themselves as '*rather* deaf', rather than having complete hearing loss, commented on the noises that bothered them: in this case, noise made with bedpans.[230] In a sense, the questionnaire format did allow for more

---

[229] DHSS, *Annual Report 1973* (HM Stationery Office, 1974), pp. 32–3; King Edward's Hospital Fund for London, 'NHS Hospital Bed Numbers', www.kingsfund.org.uk/publications/nhs-hospital-bed-numbers (accessed: 16 March 2021). There are few comparable national statistics for earlier periods, but inpatients in Glasgow in the 1880s had a similar average stay to that of the early NHS (28.8 days) and the London Gynaecological Hospital had an average stay of nine weeks in the 1860s. Gordon Douglas Pollock, 'The Glasgow Royal Infirmary: Aspects of Illness and Health Care in the Victorian City', *International Review of Scottish Studies*, 34 (2009), 107–38; W. R. Winterton, 'The Story of the London Gynæcological Hospitals', *Proceedings of the Royal Society of Medicine*, 54 (1961), 191–8.

[230] King Edward's Hospital Fund for London, *Report of a Follow-up Enquiry*, p. 21. Emphasis added.

heterogeneity than the imagined universal patient required by decibel levels. It made space for alternative definitions of 'noise' for those with limited hearing, for example, objects that vibrated and rattled. In general, however, little attention was paid to diversity of sensory perception in the surveys or reports. The New Guy's House surveys also showed that 96 per cent of respondents were over eighteen (the youngest was fourteen) and there was a fairly even gender split with a slightly higher proportion of female respondents (55 per cent).[231] The absence of younger children is significant in the making of an idea that a patient-centred soundscape was a quiet one; there were seemingly no equivalent studies at children's hospitals, where 'noise' may have had a more positive connotation.[232]

These demographic issues are extremely important in understanding the sonic ordering of space. Historians have long shown that 'noise' was often constructed in race- and class-based terms. They have identified such trends in neighbourhood disputes about 'noise', and have examined how race intersected with the uses of noise abatement legislation to regulate and control specific 'nuisances' such as blues parties.[233] Yasmin Gunaratnam has also examined noise in contemporary healthcare settings in relation to 'ethnic and cultural difference'.[234] Gunaratnam shows that healthcare 'environments can become white' through the management of sound, and that there are 'four interrelated significations of noise … noise as uncontrollable, noise as injurious, noise as suffering, and noise as "not-white"'.[235] There is little comparable work on historical hospitals, but some historians have noted similar trends in passing. Hillel Schwartz notes that elsewhere, and in the private sector, 'prosperous hospitals incorporated more semiprivate and private rooms. The better-off would no longer have to … tolerate noises they associated with lower classes,

---

[231] Out of 331 respondents who gave their gender and 316 who gave their age; LMA, 'Completed Questionnaires'.

[232] In 1960, for example, one Los Angeles hospital benefitted from a local motorcycle club's 'Project Noise', which collected radios, television and record players for children in hospital; Anon., 'Project Noise', *Los Angeles Times*, 9 June 1960, 10.

[233] Noise nuisance legislation was used to control unregulated nightlife in the post-war period, and Hansard debates show continued complaints about 'blues parties' right up to the end of the century; Hansard, HC, vol. 178, cc1023–77 (31 October 1990). There is a compelling argument that such neighbourhood noise complaints were 'racialised', though there is also evidence of neighbourhoods taking direct action instead of turning to the police; see Deborah Talbot, *Regulating the Night: Race, Culture and Exclusion in the Making of the Night-Time Economy* (Routledge, 2007), 45.

[234] Yasmin Gunaratnam, 'Towards Multi-sensory Research: Acoustic Space, Racialisation and Whiteness', *Journal of Research in Nursing*, 13:2 (2008), 113–22.

[235] Yasmin Gunaratnam, 'Auditory Space, Ethics and Hospitality: "Noise", Alterity and Care at the End of Life', *Body & Society*, 15:4 (2009), 11.

immigrants, and other races', but private rooms to resolve such social tensions around 'noise' were not common in the NHS.[236]

Occasional comments in the King's Fund sources also indicate that race, ethnicity and the perception of cultural difference played a role in the construction of 'noise'. Responses to the 1973 questionnaire, for example, included 'Asian visitors by the dozen talking loudly, walking noisily and dropping things' and 'The whole Asian family seems to come en bloc.'[237] It is also well recorded that many migrant NHS staff were confronted with hostility and racism in the post-war period, and it is possible that some of these ideas fed into complaints about the noise made by hospital staff.[238] It should, though, not be assumed that all noise complaints came from white patients. It is likely that respondents to the King's Fund questionnaires – in London hospitals – included patients of diverse races and ethnicities. These sources in theory provide an opportunity to step away from what Jennifer Stoever rightly critiques as a dominant focus on 'white-authored conceptions of "noise"' which creates a false 'dichotomy between whites as "noise abaters" and people of color as "noise makers"'.[239] Unfortunately, though, demographic factors beyond age and gender went unrecorded on the King's Fund surveys. It therefore remains difficult to unpick their roles in noise complaints.

The needs of hospital patients were specific, but they can be understood in relation to wider social and spatial discourses about respect and neighbourliness. The label of 'noise' was more commonly applied when the *listener* was ill and the *noise-maker* was well. In this context, noise was not defined in terms of the loudness of the sound but also in relation to its social symbolism. The King's Fund report in 1960, for example, included the following quotes when discussing the 'noises' that disturbed patients: 'Fitter patients getting well, talking and laughing while newly operated patients need absolute rest and quiet'; 'Inconsiderate patients who are most responsible for noise by playing of the radio and television louder than necessary'; 'Talking and noises made by other patients, usually those in convalescent state showing no or little regard for others in less fortunate state'; and, showing more sympathy for the seriously ill, 'Noises made at night by other patients receiving treatment or in pain ... are not necessarily annoying but in some cases harrowing.'[240] The space(s) of the hospital created new types of socially constructed noise, grounded in specific types of social etiquette in which the

---

[236] Schwartz, 'Inner and Outer Sancta', p. 285.   [237] Hinks, *Cruel Absence of Care*, p. 22.

[238] Roberta Bivins, 'Picturing Race in the British National Health Service, 1948–1988', *Twentieth Century British History*, 28:1 (2017), 83–109; Julian M. Simpson, *Migrant Architects of the NHS: South Asian Doctors and the Reinvention of British General Practice (1940s–1980s)* (Manchester University Press, 2018).

[239] Stoever, '"Just be Quiet Pu-leeze"', p. 148.

[240] King Edward's Hospital Fund for London, *Report of a Follow-up Enquiry*, pp. 9–10.

sickest patients were those whose needs should be prioritised. Whereas Bijsterveld's work on noise and neighbours identified a belief in the right to make noise in one's own home, the hospital ward removed such a private sonic space as an option.[241] The NHS hospital involved new types of social space in which sonic order needed to be renegotiated. Questionnaire responses brought into being one way of ordering the environment: a hierarchy of *need*, with the requirements of the sickest patients given priority.

The King's Fund surveys indicated that this sonic order was based first on the shared rights of patients to peace, rather than on the needs of staff to make 'noise' in their line of work. This idea was not automatic; it grew over time with the rise of patient-centred care and the patient-consumer. Patients also implied that some staff were noisier than others in their responses to questionnaires, often in line with an implicit hospital hierarchy. They rarely complained about doctors making noise, for example, but regularly complained about cleaners (or rather the machinery of the floor cleaner) in relation to rest times.[242] Such responses were broadly in line with letters printed in medical journals between 1955 and 1961, which complained about porters who 'bray down the resounding lift-shafts', 'energetic workmen with hammers' and ward maids who 'banged ... shouted .... hummed ... sang'.[243]

Patients surveyed by the King's Fund tended in particular to comment on nurses. As there was a significant gender disparity between nurses and doctors, a new item might be added to Gunaratnam's list: noise as 'not-male'. As one response to the King's Fund survey on New Guy's House noted in 1962: 'Sisters and Nurses do whisper, but not the Drs.'[244] The 1974 King's Fund report also noted that a patient had also complained about the fact that 'Auxiliaries and domestic staff chatter ceaselessly.'[245] Another comparable response from the 1974 report brought age into the discussion, complaining about 'Night nurses if young – quite a lot of talking and giggling.'[246] Complaints about nurses often focused on female footwear, bemoaning their 'clippety-clip' or 'heavy heeled' shoes, with only a few comparable complaints about doctors' heavy soles.[247] Similar age-based and gendered complaints were made about the footwear of visitors, for example in

---

[241] Karin Bijsterveld, '"The City of Din": Decibels, Noise, and Neighbors in the Netherlands, 1910–1980', *Osiris*, 18 (2003), 173–93.

[242] King Edward's Hospital Fund for London, *Report of a Follow-up Enquiry*, p. 11.

[243] Daniel Lamont, 'Noise in Hospital', *British Medical Journal*, 2:5244 (1961), 111; Ida Seymour, 'Noise in Hospital', *The Lancet*, 266:6880 (1955), 93; G. Struan Marshall, 'Noise in Hospital', *British Medical Journal*, 1: 5165 (1960), 61.

[244] LMA, 'Evaluation of New Guy's House', NGH/Q1.

[245] Hinks, *Cruel Absence of Care*, p. 29.   [246] Hinks, *Cruel Absence of Care*, p. 29.

[247] Hinks, *Cruel Absence of Care*, pp. 27–8.

1960: 'Visitors – especially young ones. Young women with stiletto heels tap-tapping along the wooden floor.'[248] Sound and noise can be seen as a crucial part of the gendering of space and place, reflecting and reinforcing wider social structures.[249] Societal ideas about gender roles might also have been heightened in the context of hospitals, where women in particular were expected to be considerate providers of care. The King's Fund took on some of the gendered construction of noise in their report. In 1960, they noted that 'nurses who hurry and bustle about their work generally do so because of shortage of staff and time, but there is no denying that such bustling can disturb or unsettle many patients'.[250] It is difficult to imagine the sounds of male hospital consultants being described as 'bustling'.

These responses and reports re-emphasise that language is important. A qualitative survey about the 'noise' made by nurses brought it into being as a gendered, social problem in a way not possible with the decibel measurements described earlier. The subjective and gendered aspects of noise revealed by these questionnaires built on long-held societal ideas about 'noise'. Florence Nightingale's *Notes on Nursing* had emphasised in the nineteenth century that 'unnecessary (although slight) noise injures a sick person much more than necessary noise (of a much greater amount)' and that 'a nurse who rustles ... is the horror of a patient, though perhaps he does not know why'.[251] There was also change in the late twentieth century, and an important difference between observing such phenomena (Nightingale's work is phrased repeatedly as 'I have seen') and 'noise' as described by the patient. The latter brought meaning and personal experience more clearly into view, and the method itself emphasised that 'noise' should be defined by patients rather than by staff.

The age-based and gendered tone of questionnaire responses was echoed in noise complaints elsewhere. In 1962, *QP: The Journal of the Noise Abatement Society* published one patient's complaint that, '[m]aybe one can't expect a teenage or early-twenties' nurse to understand when one doesn't like the noise. "We need a bit of noise on this ward to liven it up!" was the reply I got, when I said I thought the radio music was a bit loud.'[252] This anecdote about the radio music is a valuable reminder that some people used the term 'noise' in a positive sense, with the younger nurse apparently seeing 'noise' as positive and enlivening. It also highlights some of the tensions around sound in the hospital; who had control over the choice and loudness of

---

[248] King Edward's Hospital Fund for London, *Report of a Follow-up Enquiry*, p. 13.

[249] Feminist spatial theorists have written on the importance of paying attention to the gendered nature of space and place; see Robert T. Tally Jr, *Spatiality* (Routledge, 2013), pp. 132–5.

[250] King Edward's Hospital Fund for London, *Report of a Follow-up Enquiry*, p. 20.

[251] Nightingale, *Notes on Nursing*, p. 36.   [252] Lang, 'Our Noisy Hospitals!', p. 28.

a radio station could be an important part of power dynamics in a space. Similar complaints were made in a report in *The Guardian* in 1963 on a Birmingham hospital in which a woman 'alleged that her daughter, aged 8, asked for a radio to be turned down but ... the ward sister refused'.[253] The King's Fund ethos had seemingly not yet become widespread, because this particular patient's complaints was rejected. However, there was change afoot. Patients felt able to air their complaints, both in the hospital and through the Noise Abatement Society. The process of complaining about noise, even outside the formal structures of questionnaires, in itself was productive and helped to shape NHS values.

In the early 1960s, the King's Fund also trialled music in waiting rooms, for which they surveyed both staff and patients to compare their qualitative responses. Again these questionnaires raise some questions around power and who the soundscape was for, indicating a shift towards patient-centred sound design. Staff repeatedly indicated their dislike of the music but willingness to accept it for the sake of patients: one surveyed staff member summarised, 'I personally, don't like it, but realise that patients mostly do.'[254] Such comments indicate a subtle turn towards accepting that what staff defined as 'noise' might be of secondary importance to what patients wanted. These trends should not be overstated of course, nor the medical profession treated as homogenous. One recent oral history interview, with a former paediatric nurse, recalled a consultant in the 1970s who demanded "turn it off!" when they played music in children's wards.[255] Patients themselves also had a wide range of responses to the music, most of which were positive but some of which still labelled the sounds as 'noise'. Based on questionnaire responses, the music was played at a relatively quiet level so as not to be intrusive, and it seems that this in itself was the source of complaints. Differing from the conception of 'noise' based on loudness, some defined waiting room music as 'noise' because it was not audible *enough* to enjoy; '"Background" music is itself an abomination', one patient complained. 'One either listens or does something else.'[256]

Questionnaire responses to music were often highly personal. This subjectivity may, of course, have been drawn out by the questionnaires themselves, and there are no comparable studies of – for example – talk radio or television. It is also notable, returning to some of the comments, .that the questionnaires assumed a certain demographic of patient when they asked: 'Which sorts of background music do you think are most suitable for hospitals (e.g. orchestral; organ; piano; light classical; marches; waltzes; foxtrots; Latin American etc)?'.

[253] Anon., 'Move to Cut TV Noise in Hospitals', *The Guardian*, 3 August 1963, 3.
[254] LMA, 'Background Music', A/KE/I/01/01/009, A/KE/I/01/01/011, A/KE/I/01/01/013. Punctuation is taken from the original source.
[255] NHS at 70, Stevenson.   [256] LMA, 'Background Music', A/KE/I/01/01/009

Without closing off other options, this question gave few global options and nothing 'popular': as one respondent asked – 'Why not play the latest hit records . . . for teenage patients?'[257] These absences give some insight into who noise abatement was for, in terms of the imagined average patient, despite the diversity of those using the NHS in practice.

Some respondents pushed back against this questionnaire, by rejecting the notion of fixed musical preferences. They noted that the same music could be experienced differently depending on physical and emotional health, for example: 'When bored, music can amuse, when worried, it can irritate . . . No one type of music could fail to irritate some tastes . . . wherever possible one should be able to turn it off'; 'If very weak I couldn't listen to orchestral'; and 'The choice would of course alter with the degree of illness.'[258] These responses emphasised that listening to music was a relational act, inseparable from the individual's feelings at any given time. They also implicitly advanced a particular model of patient-centred care, which resisted 'one size fits all' design and emphasised the importance of control. They align with some of the trends that Alex Mold has identified in work on the history of patient groups and how they shaped early meaning(s) of the 'patient-consumer', before the concept was taken on by the state. In the 1960s and 1970s, Mold shows, these groups advocated for a model of the patient-consumer grounded not only in citizenship and social rights but also in 'autonomy' and 'the ability to choose'.[259] Individual patients used and adapted questionnaires to promote similar ideas. Processes of consultation about music, sound and 'noise' were not simply the outcome of new NHS values but also part of making and shaping those values.

2.4 Social Solutions

Qualitative research methods, such as questionnaires, produced a conception of noise that went beyond loudness. There were undoubtedly overlaps between the noises discussed in questionnaire responses and those identified using noise meters. However, the questionnaires discussed brought into view a 'hospital noise' that was more socially and culturally embedded than those used by architects, designers and engineers. These qualitative measurements had implications for the proposed solutions to the 'noise problem' in hospitals: when conceptualised as a social or behavioural problem, noise was tackled as such. Social and behavioural approaches to noise abatement were also commonplace

---

[257] LMA, 'Background Music', A/KE/I/01/01/008.
[258] LMA, 'Background Music', A/KE/I/01/01/001, A/KE/I/01/01/011, A/KE/I/01/01/014.
[259] Mold, 'Patient Groups', p. 511.

outside hospitals, as part of wider community strategies for reducing noise. The 1963 Wilson Report on Noise, for example, emphasised that 'sympathy and consideration' was the 'best remedy' for neighbourly disturbance.[260] The hospital noise abatement strategies discussed here similarly promoted consideration as the key to noise reduction. In the NHS hospital though, the emphasis was less on 'neighbourly' sympathy and more on staff showing consideration for the needs of patients.

The King's Fund translated its report into action with a series of posters (Figure 12), commissioned from the cartoonist Fougasse, who was already well known for the 'Careless Talk Costs Lives' wartime posters. This association may be significant in itself, as the posters sought to communicate the importance of community, consideration and collective effort just as the wartime posters had done. The posters never went so far as to declare a 'war on noise', but the continuity of Fougasse's wartime aesthetic certainly would have been familiar to many members of staff. The images were eye-catching, with the same striking red border as the wartime posters; the examples shown here were intended to catch the eye of nurses in particular, encouraging them to change their behaviours. They were even released in three batches of three, to ensure that 'familiarity shall not reduce their impact', and were displayed in corridors as well as staff common rooms.[261] These posters were designed to show that hospital noise could be easily fixed with small solutions. Some of these related to material changes, such as using lubricant oil or turning off dripping taps, in response to survey comments that identified easy-fix opportunities. These were not social solutions, per se, but they did differ from design solutions; rather than suggesting a change to new layouts or different objects/materials, these posters highlighted the benefits of constant vigilance, awareness and maintenance. Noise management was thus constructed as an ongoing process, rather than something that could simply be designed or built in a hospital.

Even objects such as hospital trolleys were conceptualised in these posters in terms of nurses' behaviour, aligning with some of the qualitative research findings of the King's Fund noise questionnaires. Complaints about trolleys had often referred to the people pushing them, or the time at which they did so, for example: 'Laundry trolleys cross the wards during rest hours. Rest periods should be respected by patients and staff' or 'the tea trolley when very early morning tea is served'.[262] The tone of such complaints fed into Kings Fund posters. The middle image states 'don't let their wheels squeak', as if this noise

[260] Bijsterveld, 'The City of Din', p. 193.
[261] Anon., 'Hospital Noise', *The Lancet*, 279:7239 (1962), 1111.
[262] Hinks, *Cruel Absence of Care*, p. 15.

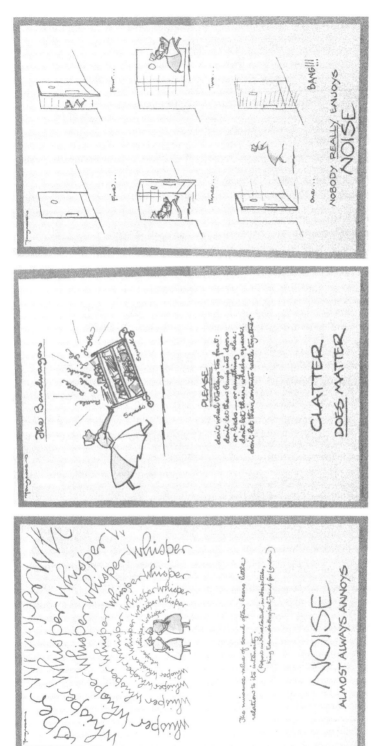

Figure 12 Posters by Fougasse for the King's Fund, c. 1958. © C. K. Bird. Reproduced by kind permission of the estate of C. K. Bird. Images provided by the King's Fund Library.

is a matter of human agency rather than a material issue. The banging doors in the third image are clearly presented in terms of a lack of the nurses' attention, while rushing around, rather than in terms of the need for a door-closer to be installed (which was presented as one solution to 'noise' as a problem of loudness, discussed previously). Quoting directly from the King's Fund report, the first poster in Figure 12 emphasises that 'the nuisance value of sound often bears little relation to its intensity'.[263] This quote, when situated alongside the whispering nurses image, neatly communicated a number of messages at once: that 'noise' was not only a problem of loudness; that women were a particular 'nuisance', due to the incessant and implicitly unnecessary nature of their 'whispers'; that the person being 'annoyed' or receiving the 'nuisance' was implicitly a patient; and that it was the nurses' duty to keep these sounds to a minimum. Such posters used visual culture to communicate the complexities of noise as a problem, and to suggest behavioural changes as a solution.

These behaviour-based recommendations were also evident elsewhere, including in reports on successful noise abatement. The King's Fund report on New Guy's House in 1962, for example, found that 'the wards ... appear quiet due mainly to good staff discipline'.[264] The Noise Abatement Society also put together some advice to 'all members of staff', though again the language implied that the advice was aimed more at nurses: '*DO* wear rubber-heeled footwear and walk lightly; answer the telephone promptly; talk and laugh quietly .... *DON'T* bustle and create a disturbing atmosphere; sing, whistle or shout; rattle keys.'[265] The emphasis on 'rubber-heeled footwear' and 'bustling' had strong echoes of the language used to describe nurses in the King's Fund research. Comments about rattling keys also implicitly related to those members of staff such as cleaners, porters or members of estates teams who required them.

Similar trends were evident in the 1961 report of the Standing Nursing Advisory Committee, based on their aforementioned qualitative survey of 'most bothersome noises'. Of particular significance is their suggestion that 'every plan for dealing with this problem must, in the first place, take into account the patients' point of view' and a repeated emphasis on staff vigilance as a noise reduction strategy.[266] This report prompted some other hospitals to undertake their own research: for example, the 'United Cambridge Hospitals'

---

[263] The 1958 report stated: 'It seemed clear that the nuisance value of a sound often bore little relation to its intensity by scientific measurement'; King Edward's Hospital Fund for London, *A Report of an Enquiry*, p. 4.

[264] LMA, 'Evaluation of New Guy's House'.

[265] Wellcome, 'Records of the Noise Abatement Society', Box 1.

[266] TNA, 'Noise in Hospitals'.

survey in the early 1960s came to similar conclusions about the importance of staff behaviour.[267] These similarities in themselves are noteworthy. Hospital-based research grounded in *subjective* and qualitative measures – particularly from the patients' point of view – tended to identify similar problems and solutions. These trends raise the possibility of a correlative relationship between qualitative research methods, definitions of 'noise' grounded in social relations and behavioural solutions focused on staff.

Questionnaires were an important part of defining noise and shaping noise abatement strategies. Again, though, it is important to avoid methodological determinism. As with those professionals who conceptualised and measured noise in terms of loudness, organisations such as the King's Fund were more likely to reach for questionnaires in the first place because they provided data that fitted with their professional remit and their care-oriented activities. Qualitative noise surveys provided a model of 'the noise problem' that over-lapped with the wider goals of the King's Fund, particularly in terms of its interest in improving NHS care. Questionnaires reinforced a model of noise as an individual, social and cultural construct, rather than just a problem of loudness. By giving space to the patient's voice, both literally and figuratively, questionnaires provided data to support a definition of noise that was grounded in meaning, rather than materiality.

2.5 The (Re)Making of Noise

Overall, this analysis supplements the work of historians of technology who, in relation to twentieth-century noise abatement campaigns, find that new methods of 'objectively' defining noise never replaced social and cultural ones.[268] Alternative ways of thinking about noise co-existed, but different groups of people leaned towards different ways of thinking about sound: the idea of noise as a quantitative, measurable problem of loudness spoke to those who worked with material solutions; the idea of 'noise' as a problem embedded in embodied and social relations spoke to those interested in patient care. New measurement tools supported, consolidated and provided data for these two different ways of conceptualising noise. Over the course of the twentieth century, one did not replace the other, but they became more firmly established – and measured – as different phenomena. These findings challenge any perception that there was a common noise abatement movement in the late twentieth century. Different groups were actually tackling in some ways fundamentally different problems, albeit under the same label ('noise') and with some areas of overlap (for example, traffic, the hospital trolley). Such ideas were brought into dialogue,

[267] TNA, 'Noise in Hospitals'.   [268] For example, Bijsterveld, 'The City of Din'.

for example, in medical research and government policy discussions, but they were conceptually very different.

3 Conclusions

Complaints about modern hospitals getting 'noisier' should not be taken at face value. Hospital soundscapes were constantly being reshaped, with the decline of some sounds and the rise of others. To think of soundscapes purely in terms of 'more' or 'less' is to lose the nuances of these changes. A focus, instead, on *qualitative* shifts to hospital cacophonies allows for more attentive listening to hospitals, past and present. Reconceptualising sound as a dynamic process, or – to return to Tim Ingold's words – a 'swirling' quality, enables historians to understand its role in shaping people's embodied experiences, social relations and hospital atmospheres. Hospital cacophonies changed over time but they also continually swirled and shifted and interacted with the air, objects and the emotions of people in hospital spaces. The hospital cacophony was not just a 'noisy' backdrop to the medical work but an active agent in the making of healthcare environments.

'Noise' also changed with every effort to measure it, and again with every effort to tackle it. Methods of measuring noise were historically contingent, changing with new technologies, shifting social relations and ideas about the sounds – or the loudness of sounds – that were 'acceptable'. The definition of 'noise' ultimately determined how the problem was tackled, in ways that would come to change the NHS hospital (acoustic engineering) and patient care (staff behaviour). These noise abatement efforts had a real impact on the structure and feel of the NHS hospital. The built environment was tangibly changed as part of noise control. Surveys of the 'noise' problem informed patient-centred thinking, rather than simply being an articulation of such thought. Ideas about who got to define and control noise, and why, fed into the particular power dynamics of the NHS hospital. 'Noise' therefore should not be abandoned as a concept, but it needs to be treated critically.

Overall, this Element has made a case for thinking beyond the 'noise problem'. It has also pointed to potential further avenues for enquiry. Its first section suggested some new historical approaches, including situating sound in (un)healthy 'atmospheres' across time and place. The second section focused on contexts in which noise was seen as something to combat, but also raised the questions of negative 'silence' and positive 'noise'. The latter issue might be particularly important in relation to specific spaces, such as children's hospitals. Indeed, there is scope for much more detailed attention to differences between types of hospital, spaces within hospitals and the people who inhabit hospital spaces. Sensory histories of hospitals would benefit from closer attention to questions of age, gender, race and class. They would also benefit from more engagement with disability histories. This work has touched upon some of these issues, but in insufficient depth and they certainly merit further study. Both sections also hinted at a need for closer examination of the grey areas between noise abatement and acoustic design. Much work remains to be done around the curation or 'staging' of hospital soundscapes, including how sound was used to elicit – or attempt to elicit – atmospheric qualities such as 'care', 'modernity' and 'homeliness'.

As a consequence of the COVID-19 pandemic, the soundscape of NHS hospitals changed dramatically while this Element was being written. Many 'non-essential' treatments were limited, reducing outpatient numbers, and hospital visiting was significantly restricted. New sounds were introduced into the hospital soundscape, with the increasing use of digital devices to connect patients to the outside world. The sensory-emotional aspects of hospital sound, and its role in the making of atmospheres, have been brought sharply into view for patients sitting in an empty hospital waiting room or receiving bad news alone. Sensory relations between people have been transformed, as speech is muffled by masks. Questions about 'silence' and what is represented by the absence of sound are at the forefront of discussions about hospital spaces. It is difficult, at the point of writing this conclusion, to anticipate the sensory future of NHS hospitals. It is possible that hospital 'noise' will be reframed and welcomed as a return to 'normality'. It is also possible that historical patterns will repeat themselves, and that noise complaints will simply return in a new form. Whatever the future brings, it is more important than ever that we listen carefully to hospital noise, sound and silence.

References

Adams, Annmarie, *Medicine by Design: The Architect and the Modern Hospital, 1893–1943* (University of Minnesota Press, 2008).

'The Spaces of the Hospital: Spatiality and Urban Change in London 1680–1820', *Journal of Architectural Education*, 69:1 (2015), 130–1.

Adams, Annmarie, and David Theodore, 'The Architecture of Children's Hospitals in Toronto and Montreal, 1875–2010', in Cheryl Krasnick Warsh and Veronica Strong-Boag, eds, *Children's Health Issues in Historical Perspective* (Wilfrid Laurier University Press, 2005), pp. 439–78.

Addis, Bill, 'A Brief History of Design Methods for Building Acoustics', *Proceedings of the Third International Congress on Construction History*, 20–24 May 2009 (Neunplus1, 2009), 1–10.

Agar, Jon, 'Bodies, Machines and Noise' in Iwan Rhys Morus, ed., *Bodies/ Machines* (Berg, 2002), pp. 197–220.

An Assistant Matron, 'Noise in Hospitals', *QP: The Journal of the Noise Abatement Society*, 1:2 (1961), 11.

Anderson, J. M., 'Noise in Hospital', *British Medical Journal*, 1:5901 (1974), 248.

Annemans, Margo, Chantal van Audenhove, Hilde Vermolen and Ann Heylighen, 'Inpatients' Spatial Experience: Interactions between Material, Social, and Time-Related Aspects', *Space and Culture*, 21:4 (2018), 495–511.

Anon., 'Ashford Hospital', *Hospital Development*, 2:4 (1974), 37.

'Casscom at the Charing Cross Hospital, Fulham', *Hospital Development*, 2:1 (1974), 12.

'Communications Systems Feature', *Hospital Design*, 9:4 (1981), 19–20.

'Cutting Down the Noise in Hospital Wards', *The Guardian*, 9 May 1935, 6.

'End Washing Up Noises in Hospitals', *The Guardian*, 1 March 1961, 10.

'Hinges Oiled', *The Jerusalem Post*, 5 September 1966, 4.

'Historical Milestones of a Sound Level Meter', www.bksv.com/en/ Knowledge-center/blog/articles/sound/sound-level-meter-history (accessed: 11 January 2021).

'Hospital Noise', *The Lancet*, 279:7239 (1962), 1111.

'Installations', *Hospital Development*, 8:4 (1980), 15.

'Milton Keynes DGH', *Hospital Development*, 12:1 (1984), 28.

'Minidata: Royal Victoria Infirmary', *Hospital Development*, 3:3 (1975), 44.

'Move to Cut TV Noise in Hospitals', *The Guardian*, 3 August 1963, 3.

'Nice Noise', *The Lancet*, 204:5283 (1924), 1139.

'Noise in Hospital', *British Medical Journal*, 4:5893 (1973), 625–6.

'Noise in Hospitals', *Chicago Daily Tribune*, 24 March 1958, 22.

'Noise in Hospitals', *The Lancet*, 272:7059 (1958), 1269.

'Noise in Hospitals', *The Lancet*, 278:2702 (1961), 590.

'Noise Near Hospital', *South China Morning Post*, 13 July 1960, 2.

'Noise Ratings', www.acousticcomfort.co.uk/uploads/Noise%20Ratings.pdf (accessed: 16 November 2020).

'Noiseless Hospitals', *British Medical Journal*, 1:3917 (1936), 220.

'Noises Off', *The Guardian*, 19 December 1960, 4.

'The Patient in His Hospital', *The Lancet*, 261:6753 (1953), 227–8.

'Patient Isolation Unit from MDH', *Hospital Development*, 13:4 (1985), 19.

'Progressive Patient Care', *British Medical Journal*, 1:1816 (1962), 1816–17.

'Project Noise', *Los Angeles Times*, 9 June 1960, 10.

'Royal Lancaster Infirmary Maternity Unit', *Hospital Development*, 4:6 (1976), 24.

'Viewpoint', *Hospital Development*, 12:9 (1984), 12.

'The Woes of a Hospital Resident', *The Lancet,* 224:5792 (1934), 513.

Ashley, Julian, *Anatomy of a Hospital* (Oxford University Press, 1987).

Atkinson, Rowland, 'Ecology of Sound: The Sonic Order of Urban Space', *Urban Studies*, 44:10 (2007), 1905–17.

Barad, Karen, *Meeting the Universe Halfway: Quantum Physics and the Entanglement of Matter and Meaning* (Duke University Press, 2007).

Barro, Senen, Jesus Presedo, Paulo Félix, Daniel Castro and Jose Antonio Vila, 'New Trends in Patient Monitoring', *Disease Management and Health Outcomes*, 10:5 (2002), 291–306.

Bates, Victoria, 'Sensing Space and Making Place: The Hospital and Therapeutic Landscapes in Two Cancer Narratives', *Medical Humanities*, 45:1 (2019), 10–20.

BBC, 'NHS Told to Ditch "Outdated" Pagers', 23 February 2019, www.bbc.co.uk/news/technology-47332415 (accessed: 8 January 2021).

BBC 'Number of UK Homes with TVs Falls for First Time', 9 December 2014, www.bbc.co.uk/news/entertainment-arts-30392654 (accessed: 17 March 2021).

BBC 'Trolley Passing in Hospital Corridor – 1966', https://sound-effects.bbcrewind.co.uk (accessed: 14 December 2020).

BBC 'Whatever Happened to Hospital Radio?', 3 September 2012, www.bbc.co.uk/news/magazine-19270013 (accessed: 8 January 2021).

Benyovsky Latin, Irena, Jane L. Stevens Crawshaw and Kathleen Vongsathorn, eds, *Tracing Hospital Boundaries: Integration and Segregation in Southeastern Europe and Beyond, 1050–1970* (Brill, 2020).

Berglund, Birgitta, Thomas Lindvall and Dietrich H. Schwela, *Guidelines for Community Noise* (World Health Organization, 1999).

Biddle, Ian, and Kirsten, Gibsen, *Cultural Histories of Noise, Sound and Listening in Europe, 1300–1918* (Routledge, 2016).

Bijsterveld, Karin, '"The City of Din": Decibels, Noise, and Neighbors in the Netherlands, 1910–1980', *Osiris*, 18 (2003), 173–93.

'The Diabolical Symphony of the Mechanical Age: Technology and Symbolism of Sound in European and North American Noise Abatement Campaigns, 1900–40', *Social Studies of Science*, 31:1 (2001), 37–70.

Mechanical Sound: Technology, Culture, and Public Problems of Noise in the Twentieth Century (MIT Press, 2008).

Bille, Mikkel, Peter Bjerregaard and Tim Flohr Sørensen, 'Staging Atmospheres: Materiality, Culture, and the Texture of the In-between', *Emotion, Space and Society*, 15 (2015), 31–8.

Bivins, Roberta, 'Picturing Race in the British National Health Service, 1948–1988', *Twentieth Century British History*, 28:1 (2017), 83–109.

Boddice, Rob, and Mark Smith, *Emotion, Sense, Experience* (Cambridge University Press, 2020).

Bourbonne, Adèle, 'Tactile Sound' in Ellen Lupton and Andrea Lipps, eds, *The Senses: Design beyond Vision* (Princeton Architectural Press, 2018).

Bridges, J. F., 'Noise Control', *Hospital Development*, 5:2 (1977), 29–31.

British Library Sound Archive, Interview with Stephanie Pennell by John Newton, 2009, Unheard Voices: interviews with deafened people project (Hearing Link), reference C1345/42.

British Pathé, 'Premature Baby Unit 1950', www.britishpathe.com/video/pre mature-baby-unit (accessed: 22 January 2021).

Bull, Michael, Les Back and David Howes, eds, *The Auditory Culture Reader* (Bloomsbury Publishing, 2016).

Burton, Richard, 'St Mary's Hospital', *British Medical Journal*, 301:6766 (1990), 1423–35.

Buse, Christina, Daryl Martin and Sarah Nettleton, eds, *Materialities of Care: Encountering Health and Illness through Artefacts and Architecture* (Wiley Blackwell, 2018).

Carnall, Douglas, 'Hospitals Warn against Stories between Storeys', *British Medical Journal*, 311:7004 (1995), 528.

Central Office of Information, *It Takes All Sorts* (1975), https://wellcomelibrary .org/item/b16784595 (accessed: 14 December 2020).

Chen, Bing, and Jian Kang, 'Acoustic Comfort in Shopping Mall Atrium Spaces: A Case Study in Sheffield Meadowhall', *Architectural Science Review*, 47:2 (2004), 107–14.

Coates, Peter A., 'The Strange Stillness of the Past: Toward an Environmental History of Sound and Noise', *Environmental History*, 10:4 (2005), 636–65.

Connor, Steven, 'Rustications: Animals in the Urban Mix', in Matthew Gandy and B. J. Nilsen, eds, *The Acoustic City* (Jovis, 2014), pp. 16–22.

Corbin, Alain, *Village Bells: Sound and Meaning in the Nineteenth Century French Countryside*, trans. Martin Thom (Columbia University Press, 1998).

Cowan, Alexander, and Jill Steward, *The City and the Senses: Urban Culture since 1500* (Ashgate Publishing Ltd, 2007).

Cresswell, Tim, 'Place', in Nigel Thrift and Rob Kitchen, eds, *International Encyclopedia of Human Geography* (Elsevier, 2009), 169–77.

Denney, Peter, Bruce Buchan, David Ellison and Karen Crawley, eds, *Sound, Space and Civility in the British World, 1700–1850* (Routledge, 2018).

Department of Health and Social Security (DHSS), *Annual Report 1973* (HM Stationery Office, 1974).

Annual Report 1977 (HM Stationery Office, 1978).

Douglas, Mary, *Purity and Danger: An Analysis of Concepts of Pollution and Taboo* (Routledge and Kegan Paul, 1966).

Edwards, F. Ronald, J. C. Richardson and P. M. Ashworth, 'Experience with an Intensive-Care Ward', *The Lancet*, 285:7390 (1965), 855–7.

Fair, Alistair, '"Modernization of Our Hospital System": The National Health Service, the Hospital Plan, and the "Harness" Programme, 1962–77', *Twentieth Century British History*, 29:4 (2018), 547–75.

Fennelly, Katherine, 'Out of Sound, Out of Mind: Noise Control in Early Nineteenth-Century Lunatic Asylums in England and Ireland', *World Archaeology*, 46:3 (2014), 416–30.

Fleming, H. A., 'Points from Letters: Hospital Noise', *British Medical Journal*, 1:6105 (1978), 115.

Gallagher, Michael, 'Sound as Affect: Difference, Power and Spatiality', *Emotion, Space and Society*, 20 (2016), 42–8.

Gandy, Matthew, 'Introduction', in Matthew Gandy and B. J. Nilsen, eds, *The Acoustic City* (Jovis, 2014), pp. 7–13.

Gesler, Wil, Morag Bell, Sarah Curtis, Phil Hubbard and Susan Francis, 'Therapy by Design: Evaluating the UK Hospital Building Program', *Health & Place*, 10:2 (2004), 117–28.

Glanville, Rosemary, Ann Noble and Peter Scher, *50 Years of Ideas in Health Care Buildings* (Nuffield Trust, 1999).

Gleeson, Sinéad, *Constellations: Reflections from Life* (Picador, 2019).

Graham, Megan E., 'Re-socialising Sound: Investigating Sound, Selfhood and Intersubjectivity among People Living with Dementia in Long-Term Care', *Sound Studies*, 5:2 (2019), 175–90.

Granberg, Anetth, Ingegerd Bergbom Engberg and Dag Lundberg, 'Intensive Care Syndrome: A Literature Review', *Intensive and Critical Care Nursing*, 12:3 (1996), 173–82.

Greenhalgh, Charlotte, 'Social Surveys' in Miriam Dobson and Benjamin Ziemann, eds, *Reading Primary Sources: The Interpretation of Texts from Nineteenth and Twentieth Century History*, 2nd ed. (Routledge, 2020), pp. 117–37.

Grbich, Carol, *Qualitative Research in Health: An Introduction* (Sage, 1998).

Gunaratnam, Yasmin, 'Auditory Space, Ethics and Hospitality: "Noise", Alterity and Care at the End of Life', *Body & Society*, 15:4 (2009), 1–19.

'Towards Multi-sensory Research: Acoustic Space, Racialisation and Whiteness', *Journal of Research in Nursing*, 13:2 (2008), 113–22.

Guttridge, William A., 'Courtyards in Hospital Planning', *Hospital Development*, 2:5 (1974), 34.

Hansard, HC vol. 618, cc1571–632 (4 March 1960).

Hansard, HC, vol. 178, cc1023–77 (31 October 1990).

Harris, Anna, 'Listening-Touch, Affect and the Crafting of Medical Bodies through Percussion', *Body & Society*, 22:1 (2016), 31–61.

Helmreich, Stefan, 'Listening against Soundscapes', *Anthropology News*, 51:9 (2010), 10.

Hickling, Robert, 'Decibels and Octaves, Who Needs Them?', *Journal of Sound and Vibration*, 291:3–5 (2006), 1202–7.

Hickman, Clare, *Therapeutic Landscapes: A History of English Hospital Gardens since 1800* (Manchester University Press, 2013).

Hide, Louise, 'The Uses and Misuses of Television in Long-Stay Psychiatric and "Mental Handicap" Wards, 1950s–1980s', in Monika Ankele and Benoît Majerus, eds, *Material Cultures of Psychiatry* (trascript-Verlag, 2020), pp. 186–201.

Hinks, M. Dorothy, *The Most Cruel Absence of Care* (King's Fund, 1974).

Hirschkind, Charles, 'Cassette Sermons, Aural Modernities and the Islamic Revival in Cairo' in Jonathan Sterne, ed., *The Sound Studies Reader* (Routledge, 2012), pp. 54–69.

Hosking, Sarah, and Liz Haggard, *Healing the Hospital Environment: Design, Management and Maintenance of Healthcare Premises* (E & FN Spon, 1999).

Hosokawa, Shuhei, 'The Walkman Effect', in Jonathan Sterne, ed., *The Sound Studies Reader* (Routledge, 2012), pp. 104–16.

Hospital Senses Collective, *Wards* (online booklet forthcoming at https://hospi talsenses.co.uk).

Hubbard, Phil, and Rob Kitchin, eds, *Key Thinkers on Space and Place*, 2nd ed. (Sage, 2011).

Hugh-Jones, P., A. R. Tanser and C. Whitby, 'Patient's View of Admission to a London Teaching Hospital', *British Medical Journal*, 2:5410 (1964), 660–4.

Hughes, Jonathan, 'The "Matchbox on a Muffin": The Design of Hospitals in the Early NHS', *Medical History*, 44:1 (2000), 21–56.

Ingham, James, Martin Purvis and D. B. Clarke, 'Hearing Places, Making Spaces: Sonorous Geographies, Ephemeral Rhythms, and the Blackburn Warehouse Parties', *Environment and Planning D: Society and Space*, 17:3 (1999), 283–305.

Inglis, Brenda, 'Wessex', *Hospital Development*, 1:6 (1973), 25–32.

Ingold, Tim, 'Against Soundscape' in Angus Carlyle, ed., *Autumn Leaves: Sound and the Environment in Artistic Practice* (Double Entendre, 2007), 10–13.

The Life of Lines (Routledge, 2015).

The Perception of the Environment: Essays on Livelihood, Dwelling and Skill (Psychology Press, 2000).

Ismail, Sadia, and Graham Mulley, 'Visiting Times', *British Medical Journal*, 335:7633 (2007), 1316–17.

Jasper, Sandra, 'Sonic Refugia: Nature, Noise Abatement and Landscape Design in West Berlin', *The Journal of Architecture*, 23:6 (2018), 936–60.

Jobson, Estelle, 'Engaging with Patients on the Hospital Soundscape', 19 November 2018, https://blogs.bmj.com/bmj/2018/11/19/estelle-jobson-engaging-patients-hospital-soundscape/ (accessed: 25 January 2021).

Kelman, Ari Y., 'Rethinking the Soundscape: A Critical Genealogy of a Key Term in Sound Studies', *The Senses and Society*, 5:2 (2010), 212–34.

King Edward's Hospital Fund for London, 'NHS Hospital Bed Numbers', www.kingsfund.org.uk/publications/nhs-hospital-bed-numbers (accessed: 16 March 2021).

Noise Control in Hospitals: A Report of an Enquiry (King's Fund, 1958).

Noise Control in Hospitals: Report of a Follow-up Enquiry (King's Fund, 1960).

Kisacky, Jeanne, *Rise of the Modern Hospital: An Architectural History of Health and Healing, 1870–1940* (University of Pittsburgh Press, 2017).

'When Fresh Air Went Out of Fashion at Hospitals', *Smithsonian Magazine*, 14 June 2017, www.smithsonianmag.com/history/when-fresh-air-went-out-fashion-hospitals-180963710/ (accessed: 8 January 2021).

Konkani, Avinash, and Barbara Oakley, 'Noise in Hospital Intensive Care Units – A Critical Review of a Critical Topic', *Journal of Critical Care*, 27:5 (2012), 522e1–e9.

LaBelle, Brandon, *Acoustic Territories: Sound Culture and Everyday Life* (Bloomsbury, 2010).

Lamont, Daniel, 'Noise in Hospital', *British Medical Journal*, 2:5244 (1961), 111–12.

Lang, W. R., 'Our Noisy Hospitals!', *QP: The Journal of the Noise Abatement Society*, 1:4 (1962), 26–8.

Langhamer, Claire, 'The Meanings of Home in Postwar Britain', *Journal of Contemporary History*, 40:2 (2005), 341–62.

Lawrence, Jon, 'Class, "Affluence" and the Study of Everyday Life in Britain, c. 1930–64', *Cultural and Social History*, 10:2 (2013), 273–99.

Lichau, Karsten, 'Soundproof Silences? Towards a Sound History of Silence', *International Journal for History, Culture and Modernity*, 7 (2019), 840–67.

Lomas, Kevin J., Renganathan Giridharan, C. Alan Short and A. J. Fair, 'Resilience of "Nightingale" Hospital Wards in a Changing Climate', *Building Services Engineering Research and Technology*, 33:1 (2012), 81–103.

London Metropolitan Archives, London, 'Evaluation of New Guy's House – Draft Documents and Circulars to Working Party', A/KE/I/01/24/060.
'Completed Questionnaires', A/KE/I/01/24/061.
'Background Music in Hospitals', A/KE/I/01/01/001-019.

Lupton, Deborah, 'How Does Health Feel? Towards Research on the Affective Atmospheres of Digital Health', *Digital Health*, 3 (2017), 1–11.

MacDonald, Julie M., and David Barrett, 'Companion Animals and Well-being in Palliative Care Nursing: A Literature Review', *Journal of Clinical Nursing*, 25:3–4 (2016), 300–10.

Mansell, James G., *The Age of Noise in Britain: Hearing Modernity* (University of Illinois Press, 2017).

Marsden, Alan, and Richard Leadbeater, 'Music: Seeing and Feeling with the Ears', in Ian Heywood, ed., *Sensory Arts and Design* (Bloomsbury, 2017), pp. 157–71.

Martin, Daryl, Sarah Nettleton and Christina Buse, 'Affecting Care: Maggie's Centres and the Orchestration of Architectural Atmospheres', *Social Science & Medicine*, 240 (2019): 112563.

McGuire, Coreen Anne, *Measuring Difference, Numbering Normal: Setting the Standards for Disability in the Interwar Period* (Manchester University Press, 2020).

Ministry of Health, *Report for the Year Ended 31st December 1953: Part I* (HM Stationery Office, 1954).

Mold, Alex, 'Patient Groups and the Construction of the Patient-Consumer in Britain: An Historical Overview', *Journal of Social Policy*, 39:4 (2010), 505–21.

Mooney, Graham, 'From Casualty Room to A&E', www.rcpe.ac.uk/heritage/talks/casualty-room-ae-history-hospital-space (accessed: 8 January 2021).

Morselli, Elisa, 'Eyes That Hear: The Synesthetic Representation of Soundspace through Architectural Photography', *Ambiances: Environnement sensible, architecture et espace urbain*, 5 (2019), 1–30.

NHS at 70 Archive, Alexa Warnes interview, NHSat70_AlexaWarnes_28052020.
Beverley Tiplady interview, NHSat70_BeverleyTiplady_14052019.
Edmund Hoare interview, NHSat70_EdmundHoare_03072018.
Joan Stevenson interview, NHSat70_JoanStevenson_09012019.
Peter McDade interview, NHSat70_PeterMcDade_14062019.
Shirley Herdman interview, NHSat70_ShirleyHerdman_02092019.

Nightingale, Florence, *Notes on Nursing* (Harrison & Sons, 1859).

Nuffield Provincial Hospitals Trust, *Studies in the Functions and Design of Hospitals* (Oxford University Press, 1955).

Pallasmaa, Juhani, *The Eyes of the Skin: Architecture and the Senses* (John Wiley & Sons, 2012[1996]).

Paterson, Mark, and Martin Dodge, eds, *Touching Space, Placing Touch* (Routledge, 2012).

Pattison, Helen M., and Claire E. Robertson, 'The Effect of Ward Design on the Well-being of Post-operative Patients', *Journal of Advanced Nursing*, 23:4 (1996), 820–6.

Payer, Peter, 'The Age of Noise: Early Reactions in Vienna, 1870–1914', *Journal of Urban History*, 33:5 (2007), 773–93.

Payling, Daisy, '"The People Who Write to Us Are the People Who Don't Like Us": Class, Gender, and Citizenship in the Survey of Sickness, 1943–1952', *Journal of British Studies*, 59:2 (2020), 315–42.

Peters, Kimberley, *Sound, Space and Society: Rebel Radio* (Springer, 2018).

Pollock, Gordon Douglas, 'The Glasgow Royal Infirmary: Aspects of Illness and Health Care in the Victorian City', *International Review of Scottish Studies*, 34 (2009), 107–38.

Pütsep, Ervin, *Modern Hospital: International Planning Practices* (Lloyd-Luke, 1979).

Radford, Philip, 'Noise – Hearing Loss and Psychological', *British Medical Journal*, 282:6257 (1981), 73.

Rauh, Andreas, *Concerning Astonishing Atmospheres: Aisthesis, Aura and Atmospheric Portfolio* (Mimesis International, 2018).

Reinarz, Jonathan, 'Learning to Use Their Senses: Visitors to Voluntary Hospitals in Eighteenth-Century England', *Journal for Eighteenth-Century Studies*, 35:4 (2012), 505–20.

Rice, Tom, *Hearing the Hospital: Sound, Listening, Knowledge and Experience* (Sean Kingston Press, 2013).

Richardson, Harriet, ed., *English Hospitals, 1660–1948: A Survey of Their Architecture and Design* (RCHME, 1998).

Rivett, Geoffrey, *From Cradle to Grave: Fifty Years of the NHS* (King's Fund, 1998).

Roberts, J. F., 'Noise and Its Effects', *British Medical Journal*, 2:5463 (1965), 702.

Rosenfeld, Sophia, 'On Being Heard: A Case for Paying Attention to the Historical Ear', *The American Historical Review*, 116:2 (2011), 316–34.

Rosenberg, Charles E., *The Care of Strangers: The Rise of America's Hospital System* (Basic Books, 1987).

Salimbeni, Alice, 'A Workshop to Reflect on a Possible Mediation between Affective and Political Atmospheres' in Damien Masson, ed., *Proceedings of the Fourth International Congress on Ambiances* (Réseau International Ambiances, 2020).

Saunders, Alan, 'The Sound of Silence', *Hospital Development*, 24:10 (1993), 39–41.

Schwartz, Hillel, 'Inner and Outer Sancta: Earplugs and Hospitals', in Trevor Pinch and Karin Bijsterveld, eds, *The Oxford Handbook of Sound Studies* (Oxford University Press, 2012), pp. 273–97.

Seymour, Ida, 'Noise in Hospital', *The Lancet*, 266:6880 (1955), 53.

Shovelton, David S., 'Reflections on an Intensive Therapy Unit', *British Medical Journal*, 1:6165 (1979), 737.

Simpson, Julian M., *Migrant Architects of the NHS: South Asian Doctors and the Reinvention of British General Practice (1940s–1980s)* (Manchester University Press, 2018).

Sloane, Robert, 'The Healing Arts', *Hospital Development*, 15:5 (1987), 38–9.

Smith, Mark Michael, ed., *Hearing History: A Reader* (University of Georgia Press, 2004).

Smith, Tony, 'Sound Masking Advances', *Hospital Development*, 14:2 (1986), 39.

Snow, Stephanie, and Emma Jones, 'Immigration and the National Health Service: Putting History to the Forefront', *History and Policy* (2011), www.historyandpolicy.org/policy-papers/papers/immigration-and-the-national-health-service-putting-history-to-the-forefron (accessed: 6 January 2021).

Soutar, Richard L., and John A. Wilson, 'Does Hospital Noise Disturb Patients?', *British Medical Journal*, 292:6516 (1986), 305.

Spence, Charles, and Steve Keller, 'Medicine's Melodies: On the Costs & Benefits of Music, Soundscapes, & Noise in Healthcare Settings', *Music and Medicine*, 11:4 (2019), 211–25.

Statham, Cecily, 'Noise and the Patient in Hospital: A Personal Investigation', *British Medical Journal* (5 December 1959), 1247–8.

Stevenson, Christine, *Medicine and Magnificence: British Hospital and Asylum Architecture, 1660–1815* (Yale University Press, 2000).

Stoever, Jennifer, '"Just Be Quiet Pu-leeze": The New York Amsterdam News Fights the Postwar "Campaign against Noise"', *Radical History Review* 2015:121 (2015), 145-68.

Struan Marshall, G. 'Noise in Hospital', *British Medical Journal*, 1:5165 (1960), 61.

Sumartojo, Shanti, and Sarah Pink, *Atmospheres and the Experiential World: Theory and Methods* (Routledge, 2018).

Sumartojo, Shanti, Sarah Pink, Melisa Duque and Laurene Vaughan, 'Atmospheres of Care in a Psychiatric Inpatient Unit', *Design for Health*, 4:1 (2020), 24–42.

Talbot, Deborah, *Regulating the Night: Race, Culture and Exclusion in the Making of the Night-Time Economy* (Routledge, 2016).

Tally Jr, Robert T., *Spatiality* (Routledge, 2013).

The National Archives, London, 'Committee on the Problem of Noise: From Public', MH 146/32.

'Noise in Hospitals', MH 146/44.

Theodore, David, 'Sound Medicine: Studying the Acoustic Environment of the Modern Hospital, 1870–1970', *The Journal of Architecture*, 23:6 (2018), 986–1002.

'Treating Architectural Research: The Nuffield Trust and the Post-war Hospital', *The Journal of Architecture*, 24:7 (2019), 982–98.

Thompson, Emily, *The Soundscape of Modernity: Architectural Acoustics and the Culture of Listening in America, 1900–1933* (MIT Press, 2002).

Toy, Isobel, 'Pawprints in the Hospital', Society for the Social History of Medicine blogs, https://sshm.org/undergraduate-essay-prize-blogs/pawprints-in-the-hospital/ (accessed: 8 January 2021).

Ulrich, Roger S., Craig Zimring, Xuemei Zhu *et al.*, 'A Review of the Research Literature on Evidence-Based Healthcare Design', *HERD*, 1:3 (2008), 61–125.

Verderber, Stephen, and David J. Fine, *Healthcare Architecture in an Era of Radical Transformation* (Yale University Press, 2000).

von Fischer, Sabine, and Olga Touloumi, 'Sound Modernities: Histories of Media and Modern Architecture', *The Journal of Architecture*, 23:6 (2018), 873–80.

Waddington, Keir, *Medical Education at St. Bartholomew's Hospital, 1123–1995* (Boydell & Brewer, 2003).

Wagenaar, Cor, ed., *The Architecture of Hospitals* (NAi Publishers, 2006).

Watt, Ben. , *Patient: The True Story of a Rare Illness* (Penguin, 1996).

Way, Rob B., Sally A. Beer and Sarah J. Wilson, 'What's That Noise? Bedside Monitoring in the Emergency Department', *International Emergency Nursing*, 22:4 (2014), 197–201.

Weber, Heike, 'Stereo City: Mobile Listening in the 1980s', in Matthew Gandy and B. J. Nilsen, eds, *The Acoustic City* (Jovis, 2014), pp. 156–63.

Webb, Katherine A., *From County Hospital to NHS Trust: The History and Archives of NHS Hospitals, Services and Management in York, 1740–2000* (Borthwick Publications, 2002).

Wellcome Library, London, 'Records of the Noise Abatement Society', SA/NAS (uncatalogued), accession number 2131.

'Environmental Assessments of Noise and Temperature in 2 Wards over 24 hours', GC/136/1/6.

Williamson, Beth, 'Sensory Experience in Medieval Devotion: Sound and Vision, Invisibility and Silence', *Speculum*, 88:1 (2013), 1–43.

Willis, Julie, Philip Goad and Cameron Logan, *Architecture and the Modern Hospital: Nosokomeion to Hygeia* (Routledge, 2019).

Wilson, Alan, *Noise: Final Report [of the] Committee on the Problem of Noise* (HM Stationery Office, 1963).

Winterton, W. R., 'The Story of the London Gynæcological Hospitals', *Proceedings of the Royal Society of Medicine*, 54 (1961), 191–8.

World Health Organization, *Noise: Executive Summary-Environmental Health Criteria 12* (World Health Organization, 1980).

Xyrichis, Andreas, John Wynne, Jamie Mackrill, Anne Marie Rafferty and Angus Carlyle, 'Noise Pollution in Hospitals', *British Medical Journal* (2018), 363:k4808.

Acknowledgements

The ideas in this Element have been in development for a number of years, with support and input from many people. The University of Bristol supported this project's development from its early days, with scoping funding from the Elizabeth Blackwell Institute and Strategic Research Fund. The International Strategic Fund allowed me to spend a month as a visiting scholar at Concordia University's Centre for Sensory Studies. The Department of History's 'creative histories' cluster recently dedicated a creative writing session to hospital noise. Conversations with a 'Hospital Senses Collective', on interdisciplinary retreats funded by the Wellcome Trust, have fundamentally shaped my thinking about materiality, space, nature, emotions, architecture and sound; two of this 'collective', Agnes Arnold-Forster and Clare Hickman, generously gave feedback on this Element. Sam Goodman also read an earlier draft for me, in the midst of finishing his own book, and I am eternally grateful for his unwavering support.

The writing of this Element has been made possible by my UKRI Future Leaders Fellowship 'Sensing Spaces of Healthcare: Rethinking the NHS Hospital' [MR/S033793/1]. My project team, advisory board and mentor have all made time to talk through ideas in a challenging year. The archives that form the basis of this research have also been phenomenally supportive, including the London Metropolitan Archives, the Wellcome Library and the Royal Institute of British Architects Library. Laura Robson-Mainwaring from the National Archives, Angela Whitecross from the 'NHS at 70' project, and the King's Fund Library team were exceptionally helpful in locating materials for me when gaining access to archives became impossible in 2020.

In writing these acknowledgements, I am reminded of how many hands and ears help to make even a short text, and how much generosity there is in academia. I have been unable to name every individual here, but if you have ever taken time to talk to me about this project, be sure that I remember and I am grateful.

Cambridge Elements ≡

Histories of Emotions and the Senses

Jan Plamper
University of Limerick

Jan Plamper is Professor of History at the University of Limerick. His publications include *The History of Emotions: An Introduction* (Oxford, 2015); a multidisciplinary volume on fear; and articles on the sensory history of the Russian Revolution and on the history of soldiers' fears in World War One. He has also authored *The Stalin Cult: A Study in the Alchemy of Power* (Yale, 2012) and *Das neue Wir: Warum Migration dazugehört. Eine andere Geschichte der Deutschen* (S. Fischer, 2019).

About the Series

Born of the emotional and sensory 'turns,' *Elements in Histories of Emotions and the Senses* move one of the fastest-growing interdisciplinary fields forward. The series is aimed at scholars across the humanities, social sciences, and life sciences, embracing insights from a diverse range of disciplines, from neuroscience to art history and economics. Chronologically and regionally broad, encompassing global, transnational, and deep history, it concerns such topics as affect theory, intersensoriality, embodiment, human–animal relations, and distributed cognition.

Cambridge Elements ≡

Histories of Emotions and the Senses

CPSIA information can be obtained
at www.ICGtesting.com
Printed in the USA
LVHW080702071221
705492LV00014B/1187